THE
BABYSITTER'S
HANDBOOK

THE BABYSITTER'S HANDBOOK

SAMANTHA WILSON

The Babysitter's Handbook
© 2004 by Samantha Wilson.
All rights reserved.

Published by Kidproof Safety

No part of this book may be used or repro-
duced in any manner whatsoever without
the prior written permission of the publisher,
except in the case of brief quotations embod-
ied in reviews.

Canadian edition published by Collins, an
imprint of HarperCollins Publishers Ltd.
Collins edition:2005

Kidproof books may be purchased for educa-
tional, business, or sales promotional use
through our Special Markets Department.

Kidproof Safety
218-1080 Mainland Street
Vancouver, BC
Canada V6B 2T4

www.kidproofsafety.com

Library and Archives Canada Cataloguing in
Publication

Wilson, Samantha, 1966–

The Babysitter's handbook / Samantha
Wilson.

ISBN-13: 978-0-00-639578-2
ISBN-10: 0-00-639578-3

1. Babysitting. I. Title.

HQ769.5.W54 2005 649'.1'0248
C2005-902446-1

TC 9 8 7 6 5 4 3 2 1

Design and layout by the Vancouver Desktop
Publishing Centre Ltd.
Colour illustrations by Lorne Carnes

Contents

For the Parents

From one parent to another, I can tell you that one of my greatest fears is whether my kids will be safe when I can't be with them. Kidproof is dedicated to all aspects of child safety, and we teach kids and parents how to look at children's safety in a positive way and without fear.

This handbook is part of our exclusive Babysitter's Training Program. This is the most comprehensive, full-bodied course available. We believe in not only teaching children and teens about safety, but also testing their knowledge to be sure that they fully understand what they have learned.

We also believe in using real life experiences from experts who know what works and what doesn't. We take safety seriously, and that is how we have become the leader in child safety education. Every person who successfully completes the Kidproof Babysitter's Training Program will be armed with the most current, valuable knowledge and skills possible.

If you are a parent of a babysitter in training, or looking to hire a babysitter, rest assured, our babysitters are the best in the biz! We set our standards high, because there is no room for compromise when it comes to child safety. Visit us online at **www.kidproofsafety.com** to learn about other programs and services that make us the leading source for child safety education.

Sincerely,
Samantha Wilson
Founder, President, Kidproof Safety.

Getting the Most out of *The Babysitter's Handbook*

Kidproof has been the leader in babysitter training and child safety programs for many years. Our programs are developed by experts in every field of safety, including law enforcement, health professionals, and child safety.

Kidproof decided that it was time for a new approach to babysitter training. Who could be better than the leaders in safety education to provide the best program available? Kidproof, of course!

The Babysitter's Handbook is packed full of advice, guides, tips, and information that is based on real life experiences from kids, and experts in the know. We get the information every babysitter needs and deliver it in an entertaining and memorable way.

Our handbook is full of easy to read tips, side-bars, problemsolving, and activities that are entertaining, useful, and will help you become a professional, safe babysitter.

We don't just talk about becoming a babysitter, we teach you how to be great a one! After reading *The Babysitter's Handbook*, you will be confident and prepared to be the best babysitter possible—professional, safe, and in demand.

As you move through the pages, pay close attention to the side-bars, which will point out the most important ideas, tips, and advice. We include problem-solving based on real events—there is nothing made up here! We top it off with definitions of some common terms and issues that babysitters face throughout their babysitting jobs.

This handbook is designed to increase your confidence and skills to make you the best babysitter possible.

Look for the notes and forms areas at the end of each chapter. These are parts of the handbook that you can write in and work through. The forms can be photocopied and should be used as templates for preparing to get a job and completing the job successfully.

Write in the handbook. Make notes when necessary. It is your guide to becoming a great babysitter.

Thousands of teenagers, both boys and girls, participate in and pass the Kidproof Babysitter's Training Program each year, using this handbook as their guide. Whether you decide to babysit or not, The Babysitter's Handbook is a fantastic way to increase child safety awareness and provide basic life skills.

Now, turn the page and let's get started making you a great babysitter!

ONE
Becoming a Great Babysitter

WOW! You want to be a babysitter? That is fantastic! Parents everywhere are jumping for joy, because one thing is certain, babysitters are always in demand.

Most moms and dads have a very hard time finding a really good babysitter—no, a great babysitter!—one that they trust is safe, confident, and able to care for their kids as well as they would. Make no mistake, becoming a babysitter is serious business. The life of a child is in your hands. What you do, or don't do, can make the difference.

In this chapter you will learn

- the legal age to babysit

- how to safely find a babysitting job

- how much to charge for your services

- how to prepare for an interview

- how to present yourself as a professional

The legal age to babysit

You must have a lot of questions running through your mind now that you and your parents have decided that you are ready to learn how to be a great babysitter. One of the first things you will need to know is how old you have to be before you can start babysitting.

Do you know?

Guess what. There is no legal age to babysit—period!

Many people believe that children must be at least 12 years old before they can babysit other children. Some people think that the legal age is different when you are babysitting brothers and sisters. This is not true. In most States there is no law that states when a child can legally babysit, and there is no such thing as a "babysitter's licence" for kids.

Here is why.

Kids mature at different speeds. Can you think of friends or classmates who act a lot younger than their age? Maybe you know some kids who are called "mature for their age." Maybe that kid is you!

The point is that because kids mature and learn at different speeds, there is no law that says you must be a certain age before you can babysit. If there was, some kids might be babysitting when they are too immature to do so.

What the law says is that all children need to be protected. That includes babysitters. Most laws say that you are a child until you are at least 16 years old. Believe it or not, some say you are still a child until you are 19! Of course, most kids can babysit much earlier than 19 years old. What is important is that you have to be able to take care of yourself and make safe choices, as well as understand the special needs of the children you are babysitting, before you are ever left alone. Parents need to be certain that both you and the children will be safe in their absence.

Often kids are ready to learn how to babysit around 11 years old. Many do not begin to babysit infants or on their own until they are well into their teens.

Can you become a great babysitter if you are 12 years old?

Sure you can. But it takes practice, dedication, and skill to be great at anything. It is ultimately up to your parents and the people who want to hire you to decide if you are ready, capable, and safe to babysit. Unfortunately, even if you think you are very mature, it is still your parents' final decision.

How to find a job

Getting a babysitting job is a lot like getting a job when you are older, with a couple of differences. As a kid, you will need to follow some safety rules before you begin your search for the perfect babysitting job.

We have already learned that great babysitters are in demand. But where can you find all the parents eager to hire you?

Before you start searching want ads in the local paper, there are some important tips you will need to know to keep safe.

Let's see if you can think of the best ways to find a babysitting job.

The best way to find a babysitting job is to go to people you already know. Spread the word with family friends, relatives, neighbours, your parents' co-workers, younger kids at your school (possibly a reading buddy in a lower grade). Tell them all that you are available and trained to be a babysitter.

Great babysitters know that safety is a top priority. They also always follow the golden rules of safe babysitting. Learn them now, and remember—they must *never* be broken.

GOLDEN RULES

1. You must always get permission from your parents before accepting any babysitting job. It is your parents' final decision whether you will be able to babysit. Make them part of the decision process.

2. Never answer or post babysitting job advertisements. It is dangerous to answer an ad looking for a babysitter. You do not know the person who is posting the ad, nor do you know the kids. *Only* babysit for family, friends, and neighbours whom you and your parents already know.

   Never place an ad or post a notice in a public area such as a library or recreation centre saying that you are available to babysit. This is very dangerous and is breaking the rules!

3. Never accept a babysitting job from someone that you don't know. *Never* register for a babysitters' group or through an organization that claims to find babysitting jobs. This service should be available only to adults, not kids. *Never* meet someone in person whom you met online if they offer you a babysitting job. The Internet is full of people who are not who they say they are.

The interview

Perfect resumés and dynamic interviews will win you the job!

For any job worth seeking and getting, you should be able to have a great interview. Just because you know the person asking you to babysit doesn't mean that you should not act like the complete professional that you can be. Not only will a great interview confirm that you are the best person for the job, it will help you prepare for job interviews in the future.

Think of the interview as not just the potential employers getting to know you—it is also a great time for you to get to know the employers and their children. This will allow you to decide if you want to babysit their kids. Part of becoming a professional and safe babysitter is being mature enough to recognize your limitations and be true to your instincts. Just because someone offers you the job doesn't mean you have to take it.

Creating a great resumé

A resumé is a document that you give a potential employer that tells them previous jobs you have done, your training, hobbies, contact information, and any other facts you feel would be important for the job you are applying for.

It is usually in a simple format that lists your name, contact information, and the objective or reason that you want the job, as well as any training you have received or babysitting experience you have. You can also mention hobbies and volunteer experience.

SAMPLE RESUMÉ

YOUR NAME
Address Line 1
City, Province, Postal Code
Phone: (000) 555-2468
E-mail: someone@microsoft.com

OBJECTIVE: To provide safe, reliable, and professional babysitting services.

QUALIFICATIONS

Use action words to maximize the impact. Describe how your background and strengths would make you a great babysitter. This should sell your best qualities. Use ideas from your Self-Assessment.

EDUCATION & TRAINING

year   Kidproof Safety's Babysitter's Training Program

year   first aid

year   List any other education you have had that is relevant to this job application.

BABYSITTING EXPERIENCE

Name of Family

Describe your previous babysitting experience. Include the ages of the children and your responsibilities.

HOBBIES

Describe what your hobbies and interests are. Use this part to really show off your fun and outgoing personality!

VOLUNTEER EXPERIENCE

Describe any volunteer experience you have had and why you think it helps you be a great babysitter.

REFERENCES See letters of reference (attached).

When you are developing your resumé, keep in mind that you are trying to sell yourself as a babysitter. Therefore only put in what you feel applies to being a great babysitter. If you haven't babysat before and you love kids—put it in your resumé! Include times that you have volunteered at school to help younger kids. All of these things show that you really love kids and want to take care of them.

Most parents feel that a babysitter training course should be mandatory before you begin to babysit. If you have not already done so, you should enroll in a Kidproof Babysitter's Training Program near you.

Tell them why you want to be a babysitter. What qualities do you have that make a great babysitter? Be sure to include your availability. Be honest and realistic. If you have a large course load at school and have a lot of extra homework, don't say that you are available all the time. A babysitting job is not the place to complete homework.

From the parent's mind:
A parent would rather hire someone they already know to babysit, and whom their kids are already comfortable with. It reduces the likelihood of the children having separation anxiety and usually makes for an easy transition into a frequent babysitting job.

Include letters of reference. These are letters from parents for whom you have previously babysat that say what a great babysitter you were for their children. If you have not yet babysat, don't worry. Get letters of reference from other people who can speak about how responsible, mature, and reliable you are. Some people to ask may be a teacher, principal, coach, or neighbour. You should try to include at least two or three letters of reference with your resumé.

Once you have completed your resumé and collected reference letters, you are ready for the interview. You don't want to have to run around collecting letters of reference at the last minute.

> If you are well-prepared, the interview will be a snap.

How do you get an interview?

Once a potential family has contacted you to talk about a babysitting job, you should first offer to set up a time for an interview. This is when you can get to know what is expected of you. Once you have set a date and time for the interview, tell the client that you will call them back once you get permission from your parents. Don't worry about the time delay. They will wait for you. Be sure to get permission from your parents first.

The night before the interview, prepare your interview package so it is ready to go. This will show your client that you are well-organized.

Interview package

- current copy of resumé

- reference letters (bring copies, not originals)

- checklist of questions you want to ask

> **TIP**
> Make sure that you have these documents done before you agree to an interview. You don't want to have to run around collecting letters of reference at the last minute.

> **TIP**
> Don't lie about your previous experience or your abilities.

Job interviews can be nerve-racking. Even when you get older and apply for jobs in the future, if you don't feel the butterflies when you are waiting for the interview, you are not the average person!

Nerves are good. They will keep you sharp and on your toes.

Be 10 minutes early and try to stay calm. An interview is a conversation. It is your chance to get to know the people who are thinking of hiring you and to talk about your qualifications to do the job. That is all. A great interview is when two people get along and answer all of each other's questions properly and professionally. Take it slowly and answer the questions the best you can.

Make sure that you don't lie about your previous experience or your abilities. Not only could you be putting yourself in an embarrassing position if you get caught in your lie, but you could be compromising the safety of the kids you babysit, especially if you are not as qualified as you say you are. Be honest with yourself and with your potential client.

After you feel that you have answered all the questions that the potential client has asked, it is your turn to ask questions. Remember, a great babysitter knows her limitations and is not afraid to say no to a situation she is not comfortable with. You can't make a clear decision if you don't have all of the information you need.

> **TIP**
> Potential sitters who are neat and prepared for an interview show the client that they are professional.

There are some specific areas that you should be sure to discuss in the interview, making sure your questions are answered before you accept any babysitting job. These are covered in the interview sheet at the end of this book. If you like, copy the interview form and take it with you to the interview. Then you will be sure not to forget anything.

How much should you charge?

Babysitting is a great way for teens to learn responsibility and make some extra money. Unfortunately, many people, adults included, are uncomfortable talking about payment terms.

Show your client that you are a professional and let them know what your babysitting rates are up front. Most parents will appreciate the information.

The typical rate for a babysitter varies depending on the community, the ages and number of children being cared for, and the length of the babysitting period. Ask around your neighbourhood to see what other babysitters are charging. You will have a basic per hour fee that applies to one child, and you will charge more per hour for extra children. You may also have a different fee if the babysitting job requires you to stay after midnight.

At the time of printing this book, the average rate of pay for a casual teenage babysitter was $5 per hour for one child, $7 per hour for two children.

TIP
You have the right to say no if you are uncomfortable about babysitting certain kids.

Most new babysitters will only babysit up to two children at a time for a couple of hours. Infants take much more skill and care. You should not be left to care for an infant alone until you are well into your teen years or a young adult.

Keep a professional balance between asking for too much money and not enough. Remember, when you set a rate with a client, it will be hard to change it later. Be fair to yourself and your client.

If after the interview the client offers you the job, tell the client that you will have to ask your parents first.

You may find that you don't want to babysit for that client. It is possible that the children may be too young, there may be too many, or you may not feel comfortable in the environment or with the people in question. When you go home, discuss your feelings with your parents and decide on a polite way to refuse the client if they call and offer you the job.

Be true to your instincts and only go with what you feel is right.

Question: What happens if after I have had an interview I don't hear from the client?

Answer: If you have not heard back from the client in a week, it is okay to give them a quick follow-up phone call to see if there is any further information they require.

There may be a variety of reasons why you have not heard back from a potential client after an interview. It is possible that they no longer need a sitter or they may have selected someone else for the job.

If the client tells you that they decided to hire another babysitter instead of you, try not to be too upset. Instead, thank the client for the opportunity to meet them and politely ask if they can suggest ways you could improve your interview or training to make you a better candidate.

Don't take it personally if you don't get the job the first time out. If you practise and keep up the search, you will succeed faster than you think!

On the other hand, if the parent likes you and feels that you have the qualifications to make a great babysitter, he or she will offer you the job.

Now that you have a job—it is time to prepare, prepare, prepare!

NOTES

_____

_____

_____

_____

_____

_____

_____

_____

_____

_____

_____

_____

_____

_____

_____

_____

_____

_____

_____

_____

_____

_____

_____

_____

_____

_____

_____

_____

_____

_____

_____

_____

_____

REVIEW QUESTIONS

1. What is the legal age to babysit ?

2. Why?

3. Who decides if you can babysit?
a. you
b. the person hiring you
c. your parents
d. As soon as you pass a babysitter's program, you can babysit anyone.
e. a, b, and c

4. If you pass a babysitter's training course, do you have a licence to babysit?
a. yes
b. no
c. depends if you have the first aid part yet

5. Name two safe ways to get a babysitting job.
a. Advertise in a library that you are available to babysit.
b. Tell younger kids you know that you are available to babysit.
c. Answer an ad in the paper.
d. Tell your relatives and family friends that you are available to babysit.

6. Name two unsafe ways to get a babysitting job
a. Put your name in the "available babysitters" list at school.
b. Place an ad in the paper.
c. Ask your parents to tell their co-workers and friends that you are available to babysit.
d. Register through services on the Internet to get a babysitting job.

7. If someone offers you a babysitting job, can you say yes right away?
a. No, you need to check your school schedule.
b. No, you need to ask your parents first.
c. Yes, if you are available.
d. Yes, if you like the family and kids.

8. Name two things that should be in your resumé.
a. your name
b. your phone number
c. two reference letters
d. when you are available to work

9. What should you take with you to an interview?
a. resumé
b. cover letters
c. a, b, and d
d. list of questions

10. When should you discuss your babysitting rate?
a. after you accept the job
b. when you are in the interview
c. after the parents return home
d. one week after the babysitting job

11. Problem solving:
You are 12 years old and have successfully passed the Kidproof Babysitter's Training Program. You have your certificate. Your neighbour calls and asks you if you can babysit her two-year-old daughter who has special needs. She is desperate for a babysitter as she has been called in to work. You do not have any experience babysitting children with special needs and don't think that you would do a good job.

What should you do?

12. DEFINITIONS

Please put the correct answer in the box provided.

☐ separation anxiety

☐ employer

☐ letters of reference

☐ client

☐ babysitter's rate

Answers:

a. letters from someone who recommends you and can speak about your experiences and skills

b. the person or people who hire you to do a job

c. the amount that you will charge to babysit

d. the person or people you hope to work for

e. excessive and persistent anxiety about being separated from one's home or parents that interferes with normal activities

NOTES

TWO
Preparing for Your Babysitting Job

Congratulations! You got the job! Good work—you obviously were well prepared for the interview and showed your client how professional you are.

Now is the time to put actions to your words and prove what a great babysitter you can be.

A great babysitter is not only reliable, professional, and safetyconscious, but also *prepared!* Remember that you must always ask permission from your parents before accepting any job. Use your Client Information Sheet and ask questions and write the answers down.

Once you have these questions answered, you can give your parents all the information they need to give their permission. If they agree, now you can say, "Yes! I would love to babysit for you!"

Immediately mark the date and time on your calendar so that you do not plan anything else for the day and time.

Learning your strengths

We can't express enough how important it is to *prepare*. When you are prepared you will respond to problems, and you will have more confidence performing the job. If you wait until

> **TIP**
> A great babysitter
> is always prepared.

the last minute to prepare, it will be obvious to the client that your heart is not in it.

Babysitting is a very serious responsibility, and you must be completely prepared for any emergency. Taking care of kids is important business and there is no room for slacking.

We talked to groups of kids between 5 and 10 years old and asked them:

"What do you think makes a great babysitter?"
Fun. Brings lots of fun games. Is nice. Plays with us. Lets us play with the toys we like. Reads us stories. Is funny. Cares about us. Likes us.

"What do you think makes a terrible babysitter?"
Talks on the phone. Doesn't play with us. Is bossy. Makes us go to bed early. Watches too much TV. Does her homework when she is over. Ignores us.

We talked to groups of parents and asked them the same questions:

"What do you think makes a great babysitter?"
Reliable. Trustworthy. Safe. Has fun with the kids. Doesn't bring her friends over. Available. Professional. Likes to babysit. Follows the rules we set out. Cleans up.

"What do you think makes a terrible babysitter?"
Too busy. Won't play with the kids. Acts like they are doing us a favour. Messy. Breaks the rules. Lets the kids do anything. Unsafe.

What are your strengths and weaknesses?

Complete the Self-Assessment questionnaire on page 46 to discover the qualities and skills that will make you a great babysitter.

The babysitter's kit

The most common answer we got from kids and parents when they were describing what makes a great babysitter was, "They played with the kids."

Think of your babysitting job as a mini-vacation for the kids. It is a fun time when the children will have a slight change of routine and get to show someone new—you—what they like and are really good at. Remember, kids love to show off and look for ways to please.

A great babysitter knows how to have fun and is always prepared, and that includes bringing along a complete babysitter's kit.

A babysitter's kit is a bag or knapsack that contains items that will help you be a great babysitter when you are on the job. It should be filled with items that are only for your babysitting jobs. Always keep basic supplies in it so that if a regular client calls you at the last minute, you are set to go in very little time!

See Chapter Three, Caring for kids of all ages, for more details on specific activities for each age group of children.

Once you have a job lined up, you will begin to prepare at least one week prior to the job starting. This should give you lots of time to pick up any supplies that you may need and to think up some fun games and activities that you can do with the kids during your job.

BABYSITTER'S KIT

Mandatory items to include:
- first-aid kit
- *The Babysitter's Handbook*
- flashlight
- pencil
- Safety Checklist, Emergency Phone List, Rules and Routines Checklist, Report Card sheet.

Extra items to include:
- age-appropriate toys, games, and books
- stickers (big and small)
- sidewalk chalk
- Play-Doh
- colouring book with crayons or markers
- construction paper
- scissors (child safe!) and glue
- activity for you to do after the kids are asleep (if applicable)

Prepare an outline of activities for you and the children ahead of time, so you have a good idea of how the babysitting time will go. Remember to schedule physical activities first and more relaxing activities before bed. Plan a craft, game, and snack. Have a couple of ideas for each so that the children can make choices; they like to know their opinions are important too!

Remember that all families have their own set of rules and their own routines. Make sure you learn what those rules and routines are. Use your Rules and Routines Checklist at the end of this handbook.

The rules and routines may be different from your family's, but you still need to respect and follow them. Keep the children to their own household rules and routines. Do not let a child do something that his parents have said is not allowed, no matter how much the child pleads with you!

Three-step preparation plan

One week before

• Check contents of your babysitting kit. If you are babysitting new kids, be sure to include games that are age appropriate and that may not be part of your regular kit.

• Make copies of all forms needed, including your Safety Checklist, Rules and Routines Checklist, and Report Card.

• Call the client to confirm that you are still required and ask if there have been any changes to the plans regarding times and so on.

Two days before

- Remind your parents of your babysitting job. Make sure that you have provided them with the details of the arrangement—the time you will be babysitting until, how you will get home, and a contact name and phone number.

- Organize your homework. Make sure you are caught up so that you can take the night off to babysit (if it is during the week).

- Tell your friends that you are not available that night. Do not give them the phone number for your job, because you should not talk on the phone while you are working.

- Review your interview and follow-up questions. Make notes for any questions that you will still need answered the day of the job. For example, if you have not asked what time the children go to bed or if they have any routines, then make a note and be sure to get the answer from the parents before they leave.

Day of the job

- Show up at least 15 minutes early. If this is the first time that you are babysitting for the family, request that you come about a half-hour earlier than needed. The parents will have more time to walk you through the house and explain the rules and guidelines that you need.

- Complete the Safety Checklist and Rules and Routines Checklist.

- Review your emergency contact list. Be sure to get the phone number where the parents will be or information on who to contact in the case of an emergency.

- *Have fun!*

Problem Solving:

What if the parent is in a hurry and does not take the time to let you know of the safety hazards or concerns of the kids? What can you do?

_____

_____

_____

_____

_____

_____

_____

_____

Report Cards

A great babysitter keeps track of all the important events that happen while the parents are away. Your client will be impressed when you leave with them a full report of your and the kids' activities. Review the Report Card with the parents when they get home. Make copies of the blank Report Card so that you will have one for all your babysitting jobs.

A sample Report Card can be found in the Forms section at the back of this handbook.

After the job

Keep the Safety Checklist and Contact Information, as well as any other information regarding the family. Make your own notes about the babysitting job too. Keep all of the documents in a binder or file folder so that you will have the information if you babysit for the same family again.

NOTES

_____

_____

_____

_____

_____

_____

_____

_____

_____

_____

_____

_____

_____

_____

_____

_____

_____

_____

_____

_____

_____

_____

_____

_____

_____

_____

_____

_____

_____

_____

_____

REVIEW QUESTIONS

1. What information do you need if you are offered a job?
a. where the job is
b. what time it starts and ends
c. how you are getting to and from the job
d. how much you will be paid and how many kids you are babysitting
e. all of the above

2. Name three things that kids think make a great babysitter.

Fun, Kind and full of enery

_____

_____

3. Name three things that parents think make a great babysitter.

Trustworthy, Celieb

_____

_____

4. What items should go in a babysitter's kit?
a. first aid kit
b. toys and games that are age appropriate
c. both a and b
d. your homework

5. It is okay to tell your friends to call you at your babysitting job.

a. no

b. if the parents say it is okay

c. yes

6. What should you include on the Report Card to parents?

a. any problems with the children

b. any safety hazards

c. if anyone came to the door or called

d. all of the above

7. Problem Solving:

You have accepted a job to babysit for a new client and child. You show up half an hour early as suggested so that you can go over the routines and rules of the house. But when you get there, the parents are running late and have no time to talk to you about the routines or safety issues. You have never babysat for them before. What should you do?

_____

_____

_____

_____

_____

_____

_____

_____

8. DEFINITIONS

Please put the correct answer in the box provided.

☐ babysitter's kit

☐ emergency contact form

☐ Safety Checklist

Answers:

a. a bag or knapsack full of items that you will need on your babysitting job

b. a list of emergency numbers and contact information you will need from the parents

c. a list of safety related items that you check when you get to the client's house

PREPARING FOR YOUR BABYSITTING JOB

Self-Assessment

What is going to make you a great babysitter? Use this self-assessment to discover your specific interests and skills that will prepare you to babysit and be a great babysitter!

1. When I think of being a babysitter, I know I am best at

Caring for the kids.

2. I need to practise being better at

Making sure the kids go to bed on time.

3. I know how to

☐ care for babies

☐ care for toddlers

☑ care for preschoolers

☑ care for school-aged children

4. I also know how to

☑ choose age-appropriate games and activities

☑ choose age-appropriate meals and snacks

☑ check for safety hazards

☐ apply basic first aid skills

5. I still need to learn how to

Care for babies, Care for toddlers, how to cook meals.

6. I would prefer to babysit the following ages of children:

- [ ] baby
- [ ] toddler
- [x] preschooler
- [x] school-age

7. My biggest fear about babysitting is

loseing the kids.

What I can do about this fear:

Keep a close eye on them

8. What I am most looking forward to about babysitting is

being with kids.

_____

_____

_____

NOTES

THREE
Having a Successful Babysitting Experience

Knowing your job

It is important for a babysitter to know what each child is capable of and what to expect from children from each age group. Each age has its own set of characteristics. We have offered tips for working with these characteristics to make yours a successful and positive babysitting experience.

Caring for kids of all ages

You will need to learn different skills to properly care for kids of all ages. For example, skills you need to know for taking care of a baby include handling, diapering, feeding, and dressing the baby. As well, you need to know ways to get babies to go to sleep, and also safe toys and activities to keep them active during playtime.

Children of all ages have their own specific characteristics, and therefore their own specific needs when it comes to feeding, dressing, naptime or bedtime, and safe games and toys.

As you gain experience, you will likely have the opportunity to babysit kids of all ages. When you first begin, you will likely care for toddlers and school-aged kids.

You will usually not care for an infant until you are much more experienced. Great babysitters know their limitations and never agree to babysit a baby if they are not completely prepared and up to the task.

SUGGESTION
A great way to gain valuable experience babysitting is to ask family or friends if you can babysit for them for a few hours while they are still at home. You will take full responsibility for the kids just as if you were babysitting alone, but will have the security of the parent close by.

You may already know that children need different things depending on their ages. A great babysitter is prepared to handle each age group and understands their specific needs, concerns, and abilities.

Children have personalities, quirks, likes, and dislikes that are unique to each of them. Sometimes it is hard to figure out what makes them happy or upset. If you learn how to talk to kids of different ages and understand that their needs are unique, you will be better prepared to handle these otherwise frustrating situations.

A great babysitter is a great communicator. Let's face it, a happy kid makes a happy parent and a happy babysitter!

Babies (0–1 year old)

Many new babysitters will not take on the responsibility of caring for a baby until they are well into their teens. However, you may have a baby sister or brother whom you will need to help out with.

Babies have special needs and are completely dependent on others to survive. Babies need to be held and to feel that they are loved and not alone. If you intend to care for an infant, plan on spending one hundred percent of your time and attention on the baby.

No two babies are alike. Although they are all cuddly and cute, they also have personalities of their own. Some may love to be held, others may want to sit alone and watch the world go by. Great babysitters know that they have to change their tactics for each baby they take care of, and take the time to learn about what each baby likes and dislikes.

The best way to learn what the baby likes and doesn't like is to ask the parents. New mothers will be more than willing to talk for hours about their little bundle of joy! Don't be afraid to ask lots of questions. You will not look unprofessional. In fact, parents will feel more confident in your abilities if you show them how dedicated you are to your job and their baby.

There are some additional questions on the Rules and Routines Checklist that you should ask the parents in order to make sure you are taking the best care of their baby.

BABIES

Specific baby questions to ask the parents
(found on Additional Rules and Routines checklist)

What do I feed the baby?

Where do I feed the baby?

When do I feed the baby?

Is the baby a fussy eater? What do I do if the baby makes a fuss when eating?

Is the baby teething? What do I do for that?

What is your diapering routine?

What do you do for a diaper rash?

COMMON CHARACTERISTICS OF BABIES
- require constant attention and supervision
- can't talk to tell you what they want
- can communicate only by crying, smiling, cooing, or turning their heads away
- love games like peekaboo or quietly clapping hands
- like you to smile at them

Picking up a baby

Gently slip one hand under the baby's neck and spread your fingers to support the head and neck. Place your other hand under his bottom. Slowly lift the baby up and bring him close to your body. Wrap your arms around the baby like a cradle and rest the baby's head in the bend of your arm. Always hold him gently, close to your body.

Holding and carrying a baby

Babies are top-heavy. This means that their heads are usually heavy and hard to hold up. Most babies don't start holding their heads up without support until they are about six months old. When you hold a baby you need to support the back of her neck and head, especially if she can't support it herself. Always talk softly and quietly to a baby and move slowly. You don't want to frighten the baby.

You can gently rock the baby in your arms slowly. Never toss a baby in the air, even in play.

Some babies love to be rocked and talked to, some would rather sit on their own and watch you, and some would rather you hold them up so they can look around and behind you.

If you want to change positions from cradling the baby in your arms to holding the baby over your shoulder, gently support the head and slowly lift the baby up until he is looking over your shoulder. Keep supporting the baby with one hand under his bottom. Babies may involuntarily throw their heads back, so be sure to always keep your hand gently supporting the head and neck.

> **TIP**
> Never toss a baby in the air, even in play.

Never eat or drink anything hot while holding a baby. You need both hands to properly hold a baby and to support her head and neck. Also, you could seriously burn a baby if you spilled a hot substance on her.

Diapering

Remember we said that babies can be messy little things? Well, here is the best part—or, should we say, the part that really stinks!

Of course you know that babies wear diapers, but did you know that there are different kinds of diapers? Get the parents to show you where they keep the diapers and changing supplies before they leave. You can even ask them to show you how they diaper their baby. It could prevent a messy and uncomfortable problem in the future.

When to change a baby's diaper

You should check to see if a baby's diaper is soiled after she eats, or when she wakes up from a nap. Typically these are the times that diapers will need to be changed.

TIP

Have the parents show you how they diaper their baby before they leave.

You should also check to see if the baby's diaper is wet or dirty every couple of hours. It is best to keep a clean, dry baby than to wait until his diaper is full. Not only is a soaking diaper very unpleasant for you and the baby, but it is not very good for his bottom to be sitting in wet or soiled diapers.

You don't need to take the diaper off to check if it is wet or soiled. Many times you can gently touch the outside padding of the diaper and feel if it is heavy, and, of course, smell can be a clear sign.

How to change a baby's diaper

When it's time to change the baby's diaper, get everything you need before you start the project. First, put the baby in a safe place like crib, portable car seat, safety seat, playpen or a cradle while you are preparing the diapering area. If there is a possibility that the infant will be able to pull themselves up or out of the cradle (as some cradles have low railings), use one of the other options.

Many parents use diaper-changing tables. These are usually in the baby's room and have all of the supplies you need close at hand.

If you feel comfortable using a diaper table, remember that just because there are rails, it does not mean that you can leave the baby unattended. Babies can roll over quickly or wiggle off a table with ease.

We suggest that you choose a clear, clean, soft part of the floor to change the baby's diapers. This way you will not take the chance of the baby rolling off a table.

TIP

A clean baby is a happy baby.

Place a clean towel on the carpet or change table and set up the supplies you will need: two diapers (in case you tear one), wipes, and any cream or powder that the parent has told you to use. Keep the baby in the crib, playpen, or safety seat while you prepare the area.

TIP
Never leave a baby unattended on a change table.

Once you have everything at arm's reach, it is time to get to the dirty work and change that diaper!

Steps for diapering:

1. Gently lay the baby on his back. Make sure that he does not have anything in his hands.

2. Undo the dirty diaper by removing the tabs, then gently lift the baby by his ankles just high enough so that you can slide the dirty diaper off without spreading the mess onto the baby.

3. Move the dirty diaper out of reach of the baby. Just leave it until you are finished cleaning and re-diapering the baby.

4. Clean the baby with baby wipes or a warm cloth by wiping from front to back so that you don't spread any infections. Make sure that you dry the baby's bottom well. This will help prevent future diaper rash.

TIP
If you are changing a boy, cover the penis with a small cloth to prevent the baby from urinating on you while you clean him.

5. If there are any creams or powders that the parents advised you to use, put them on after you have cleaned and dried the bottom.

6. Slide the clean diaper under the bottom while lifting the baby's heels slightly. The tabs to the diaper should be about hip level facing you. If you are using cloth diapers, the padded part should be at the back for girls and at the front for boys. Put the plastic pants over the cloth diaper once it is fastened.

7. Fasten the tabs securely, not tightly, around the baby's tummy.

Lift the baby back into a safe place (crib, playpen, safety seat) and dispose of the dirty diaper as the parents advised. Make sure that you put away all diapering supplies, since many products can be very harmful if eaten by the baby.

Once you have the area clean, wash your hands. It is a good idea to gently wipe the baby's hands as well. Clean hands are the best way to prevent the spread of germs and disease, and babies love to put their hands in their mouth!

Congratulations! You now have a sweet-smelling, happy baby! Time to play!

Cloth or disposable diapers?

Most parents use disposable diapers, but more often now, parents are choosing to use a cloth diaper to be more friendly towards the environment.

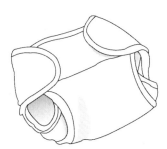

Most cloth diapers are already cut to the shape of a diaper, which makes them quite easy to use. Many even have Velcro tabs so there is no need to use safety pins.

If the baby wears cloth diapers with pins, make sure that you have the parents show you exactly how to use them. Practise changing the diaper with the parents' supervision first. Disposable diapers are the easiest, as they are pre-shaped and have removable and adjustable tabs.

Bathing a baby

We do not recommend that babysitters give a baby a bath. It takes practice and confidence to safely bath an infant, and is best left up to the parents. If for some reason the baby becomes very dirty either from a soiled diaper or eating, use a warm damp cloth to clean the baby. Do not place the baby in a tub of water. Let the parents know when they return and they may choose to bath the baby themselves.

Feeding a baby

Babies can't eat the same foods as older children. Many don't have teeth and can't chew. Small pieces of food can easily choke a small baby.

If you are required to feed the baby while you are caring for her, be sure to review the task clearly with the parents before they leave.

By bottle

Infants up to three months old will usually feed only on formula or breast milk through a bottle. Parents will likely pre-make the bottles so you will not have to worry about mixing formula. Make sure that you are prepared and ask lots of questions.

You should not carry the baby around while you are busy warming bottles and setting up the supplies you will need to feed her. Before starting to prepare for feeding time, be sure to put the baby in a safe place.

Some safe places to put the baby while you are preparing her food are

- The crib
- Portable car or safety seat
- Cradle (keeping in mind the height of the railings)
- Playpen

Find a place where you can still see the baby.

Always wash your hands before handling food, bottles, or anything that can go into a baby's mouth. This is the best way to prevent spreading germs, because babies can catch germs more easily than you!

Formula or milk needs to be warmed to lukewarm temperature. Ask the parents how they warm the bottle and write down the instructions so that you don't forget. *Never* use a microwave to warm a baby's bottle. Microwaves cook unevenly and there can be hot spots in the milk that can scorch or burn the baby badly. Microwaved foods can be cool on the outside but very hot on the inside. Don't microwave water; there must always be something in the water before you microwave it!

Ask the parents how they would like you to heat the formula. Once the bottle is ready, gently shake it to be sure that the formula is warmed evenly.

> **TIP**
> Give a baby only food that the parents have told you is permitted.

To test the temperature, gently shake the bottle so a couple of drops touch the inside of your wrist. This is a very sensitive part of your arm and a great way to test for temperature.

When you are ready to feed the baby, set up everything that you will need within arm's reach. Pick up the baby and hold him in the cradle position while you are sitting in a comfortable chair.

Turn the bottle upside down so the milk fills the bottle nipple. Gently touch the baby on his cheek with the nipple. The baby will know that you are feeding him, and will turn his head and start to suck on the nipple. You can also simply place the nipple on the baby's mouth, and if he is hungry, he will start to eat.

> **TIP**
> Always test the formula's temperature before giving it to the baby. You will know that the temperature is lukewarm when you don't notice much difference between the formula and the temperature of your skin.

Some babies won't take the bottle easily. If the baby cries or pushes the bottle away, try gently rocking him to calm him down, and try to feed him again in a few minutes. Some problems may be that the nipple may be clogged, he may need to burp, or he may not be hungry.

Never force a bottle or any food into a baby's mouth. If the baby simply will not eat, make note of it on the Report Card and advise the parents when they arrive home.

Some babies may experience separation anxiety because you are there rather than their mommy, or because their routine is different. Some babies do not like change. Make sure that you are sensitive to this, and don't panic if they don't eat or only drink a partial bottle.

By spoon

Babies who are older than three months may be starting to eat infant cereal or mashed soft food. If you are asked to feed the baby soft food, make sure that you get clear directions on what to feed and when.

Many types of cereal or foods need to be warmed up to the same temperature as bottles—lukewarm. Do not use the microwave, as it creates hot spots.

Place the food in a small bowl and then into a larger bowl of warm water and gently stir the food as it warms up. Test the temperature by dropping a small amount on the inside of your wrist.

Place the baby securely in her high chair or safety seat, and be sure to do up the seat belt. Once you have the food prepared, use a small rubber-ended spoon to feed the baby.

Many babies will eat only small bites and take quite a while to finish their food. Use this time to enjoy the experience of feeding babies. At this age it is perfectly fine for the baby to get food all over her face! If she doesn't finish, don't worry. Note it on your Report Card to the parents.

Burping

As funny as it is to hear someone burp, babies need to burp to get rid of any excess air that they swallowed while they were drinking the bottle. If they don't burp, they can get a sore tummy and become quite fussy.

Babies that have a hard time with gassy tummies are colicky. Ask the parents before they leave if the baby has any trouble burping or if she vomits easily.

After a baby is finished drinking his bottle, she will need to be burped.

Place a cloth over your shoulder and change positions to hold the baby on your shoulder. Support her bottom with one hand and gently pat the baby on her back until you hear a burp. Many babies will require burping halfway through a feeding. You can return to the feeding if the baby is still hungry.

Babies can be messy! Not only do they poop in their diapers, they also burp, spit, and vomit. Cute, aren't they? Actually, babies do all of these body functions for good reasons, not just to be gross!

Some babies will vomit part or most of their food shortly after eating. This can be completely normal. When you are burping the baby, be sure to drape a cloth over your shoulder in case she spits up or vomits.

If the baby vomits continuously, is warm to the touch and very upset and cranky, treat this as an emergency and immediately call the parents. Otherwise, be prepared to get a bit of spit-up on you—it is a dirty job, but a great babysitter doesn't mind!

Getting a baby to sleep

After all that food, diaper changing, and play, the baby will be very tired. Some even fall asleep while they are eating! The baby may give you signs that he is sleepy. He may get fidgety, start to cry, rub or roll his eyes. If you see these signs or if the baby has already fallen asleep, you should place him in his crib for a nap.

If a baby is fussy and it is time for a nap, be sure to follow his usual routine as closely as possible. Refer to your Rules and Routines Checklist that you completed with the parents to note what bedtime ritual works best. Try to follow the routine that the parents have explained as best you can. Remember, the baby will know that you are not Mommy, so don't worry if he fusses a bit at first. The change alone can cause anxiety for some babies.

When it comes time to give the baby a nap, slow down the activities, speak softly, and try to soothe the baby into a slower pace. It will be much more difficult for the baby to sleep if you are playing happily or if the baby is excited. He would much rather be entertained than miss something by sleeping. Turn down any radio, TV, or other noise and sit with the baby in a quiet, comfortable place. It is a good idea to find a place that is close to the crib or bassinet so that if the baby falls asleep, you don't have far to carry him.

Safe sleeping positions

Put the baby to sleep on her back to prevent SIDS (Sudden Infant Death Syndrome). Never put her on a waterbed, beanbag chair or soft blanket that could cover her face.

If the parent directs you to put the baby to sleep on her side, ask them to show you the position that they want you to put the baby in when she goes to sleep.

Many parents fold a blanket and prop it behind the baby's back or use a foam wedge to make sure that she does not roll over onto her tummy.

Take away all toys, stuffed animals, and anything that could harm the child from inside the crib before you place her in it. Although it may look cute to see a baby hugging a stuffed bear while she sleeps, it can easily suffocate a baby if it becomes wedged between the crib wall and the baby's face.

If the baby insists on her favourite toy to fall asleep, let her have it, but be sure to remove it from the crib when she has fallen asleep. Once you have the baby asleep and in her crib, be sure to turn down any TV or radio that you may have on if you haven't already. You will need to be sure that you can still hear the baby when she wakes up.

Some babies take only short naps. You must check on the baby every half-hour to be sure that she is comfortable and safe. Most parents use some form of baby monitor. Be sure that it is turned on and carry the receiver with you at all times.

Playtime with baby

Babies love attention and respond to musical sounds, rattles, and squeaks, usually with glee. The best time to sit and play or entertain the baby is after feeding and changing him. Be sure to follow the guidelines for appropriate toys for infants.

Infants can usually grab and hold onto large, smooth objects, but their hand-eye control can be challenged. Remember this when the baby is holding a toy. He can easily hit himself in the head with it involuntarily. Be sure to give him only large, soft toys and nothing that can come apart in pieces small enough to fit into his mouth. You don't want the baby to choke.

Keep the toys clean. Everything goes into a baby's mouth. If the baby drops a toy, be sure to wash and rinse it off before giving it back to him. Have the parents show you what toys are the baby's favourites.

SAFE TOYS AND ACTIVITIES FOR BABIES

- soft chew rings

- baby play gym

- baby bouncer seat with mobile

- blocks or large toys that cannot come apart into smaller pieces

- books with different textures

- squeaky toys and rattles

- hand puppets and stuffed animals. Make sure there are no loose buttons, eyes, or any other materials that a baby could choke on.

Toddlers (1–3 years)

Toddlers are very busy little people who need constant supervision. There is no better way to watch kids than to be part of their activities. Play with them! They love to make things, and to build things. Toddlers also like doing what you are doing, so if you are washing dishes, let them help out!

Toddlers have some special care needs as well, so be sure to ask the following questions to get specific answers about those needs.

Specific toddler questions to ask the parents
(found on Additional Rules and Routines checklist)

Is the toddler still in diapers or toilet training?

If he's still in diapers, what is the diapering routine?

If he's toilet training, what is the toilet routine?

Are there any problems with bedwetting?

Where are the clean bedding and clothing kept?

COMMON CHARACTERISTICS OF TODDLERS
- love to run and climb
- love to play games
- like to open cupboards and drawers
- like to explore and are very curious about everything. (This can be good, because it makes for a fun and busy babysitting day, but it can also be a concern because toddlers have no idea about safety!)

Diapering toddlers

Many toddlers wear diapers. Some wear them throughout the day, and older ones may only wear a pull-up diaper when they go to bed. There is a difference between diapering a toddler and a baby—the toddler can run away while you are changing her diaper!

> **TIP**
> The best way to supervise toddlers: play with them!

If you need to change a toddler's diaper, tell her that it is time to change her diaper. You can turn it into an activity by asking the toddler to get the diaper and supplies that you need.

Often toddlers can get their own diapers. This is fine, but don't let them use powders or creams on themselves. If the parents request that you use powder or cream, explain to the child that she needs to lie still while you are applying it.

> **TIP**
> Remember, it is the friction of rubbing your hands together that helps get rid of germs, not simply the soap. Take a moment to rub your soapy hands together before rinsing them.

You can use baby wipes or a warm damp cloth to clean their bottoms. Remember to wipe from front to back to avoid spreading infections.

Many toddlers will have bowel movements that are solid rather than loose and watery like a baby's. You can dump the contents of the dirty diaper into the toilet and dispose of the rest of the diaper as you would regularly. Be sure to wash your hands after you finish changing her. Have the toddler wash hers as well.

Most preschoolers can eat, dress, and use the toilet by themselves. You may find that some still wear a diaper at night but use the toilet during their wake time.

Using the toilet

Many toddlers will use the toilet and wipe their bottom without assistance. Be sure to ask the parents before they leave if the children need any help using the toilet. Some kids are very private and could be quite upset if you open the door while they are on the toilet. Others will want you close by in case they need you.

Feeding a toddler

If you are asked to feed the toddler while you are babysitting, ask the parents what they would like the child to have. Don't forget to ask about allergies and dislikes. Kids like to make choices, and toddlers are no exception; let them choose between a couple of safe snacks. They will enjoy making the decision.

Always wash your hands before and after handling any food, and make sure the child washes his hands as well. Check the temperature of any foods that require heating up. It is best to choose snacks that do not need any cooking, or ones that you can do quickly in the microwave.

Your primary safety concern will be to make sure that the toddler does not choke. When you get ready to feed the toddler, buckle him safely and securely into his high chair. Never leave him unattended. A high chair is not a safe place to put a toddler when you are busy preparing the meal. Make sure that the high chair is not within reach of dangerous items such as knives or the stovetop.

Toddlers will likely have teeth and be able to chew food. Cut the food into bite-sized pieces that are easy to chew, and always supervise a toddler while he is eating.

Be sure that he does not bounce around when he eats, as food can easily get stuck in his throat and cause him to choke.

Be sure to clean up after the snack, and get him to help out as well.

Bedtime for toddlers

Ask the parents if they have a bedtime routine and try not to change it. Don't worry, though, if the toddler will not go to sleep easily. She may just be excited to be with you!

Although you may think that if you tire a child out by playing with her she will fall asleep, this is not the case. Toddlers love to play, and if they are having a great time they may not want to stop, slow down, and go to bed.

When it is time to get the toddler to sleep, choose a quiet, calming activity like reading a story, rocking in a chair, or rubbing her back. This will help calm and relax her, which will ultimately help her get to sleep.

Problem Solving:

It is Bobby's bedtime and he does not want to go to sleep. You have tried to keep him calm, read him stories, and followed the routine as much as possible, but as soon as you put him in bed and turn out the light, he gets up and insists on sitting up until his parents get home. What can you do?

_____

_____

_____

_____

_____

_____

_____

_____

Playtime with toddlers

Toddlers love to keep busy. A great babysitter knows how to entertain children while keeping them safe. Make sure that your babysitting kit is full of age-appropriate toys and games like stickers, crayons, and colouring books that toddlers will find fun. You may need to explain to them that these are your toys and that you will be taking them with you when you leave. Most toddlers love stories and games that include activity. Plan ahead and include a variety in your kit.

Toddlers love to put things in their mouth, nose, and ears. That is why it is important that they do not play with or have access to small objects. This includes toys that can easily come apart. A pencil eraser can end up in a toddler's nose in seconds! This will surely mean a visit to the doctor. The best way to keep a toddler safe is to examine toys and remove any objects that he might choke on or put inside his body. Use the toilet-roll test to determine objects that are too small for a toddler to play with or to be within their reach.

Play with the toddler as much as possible. Not only does this make you a fun and great babysitter, it is also the best way for you to keep an eye on him and keep him safe!

SAFE TOYS AND ACTIVITIES FOR TODDLERS
- colouring books and crayons
- stuffed animals
- big picture books
- singalong songs

Preschoolers (3–5 years)

This age group can be fun and also quite challenging. Many preschoolers have very clear ideas of what they like and dislike, and what you should be doing as a babysitter.

Preschoolers love individual attention—keep this in mind if you are babysitting this age group with an older sibling. They also like to make decisions, so give them choices when picking a snack or activity.

TIP
It is a good idea to have the parents explain the rules in front of the preschooler so he knows that he can't fool you later.

Use activities to entertain them. Preschoolers enjoy doing puzzles and playing with a ball. They like to pretend to dress up, and may want you to play pretend with them as well. Have fun with it!

Feeding a preschooler

Preschoolers are likely to have many of their baby teeth and can therefore eat many of the foods you do. However, it is important to remember to keep food cut into small bite-sized pieces and have the children sit down while they eat. Preschoolers are quite busy, and it can be a choking hazard if you allow them to move around and play while they eat.

COMMON CHARACTERISTICS OF PRESCHOOLERS
- can talk
- can do some things independently, but still need to be supervised
- can use the toilet on their own

Preschoolers love finger foods, so be sure to give them fun foods that are healthy and, of course, approved by the parents. Avoid hard or chewy foods like carrots and meat, as they can become a choking hazard.

SAFE TOYS AND ACTIVITIES FOR PRESCHOOLERS
- Play-Doh
- markers
- stickers and sticker books
- construction paper
- paint (non-toxic)
- sidewalk chalk
- books
- rubber ball (they like to bounce them!)
- puzzles
- dress-up clothes (they like to pretend and may want to play house—play with them!)

Playtime with preschoolers

Preschoolers are curious and can be demanding. They require constant supervision. They understand what no means and will often challenge it. Be sure to set out the rules and guidelines clearly, and stick to your decisions. Then have fun and play!

Preschoolers love active games, and anything physical. Be sure to include appropriate safe toys in your kit to surprise them with something different from their regular toys.

Bedtime for preschoolers

Preschoolers will have definite routines for bedtime. Clarify the routines with the parents before they leave, and have them explain the bedtime routine to you in front of the children. This will ensure that the routine does not change when the parents are not there. Follow the bedtime routine and you will have a much easier time putting preschoolers to bed.

School-age (5 and older)

This is a great age to babysit, especially for a new babysitter. Most school-aged kids already have an established routine, likes, and dislikes. They communicate their feelings quite easily and may even have hobbies and interests that you can share when you are with them.

It is a good idea to learn as much as you can about the children you are babysitting before you begin. That way, you can pack your babysitter's kit with items that you know will interest and excite the kids. Remember, one of the top things that kids think makes a great babysitter is one who plays with them!

This age usually looks up to older kids, especially teenagers. It is important that you set a good example by your actions and reactions to them and your surroundings. Always be fair and positive. Do not tell them what to do, but rather make suggestions so that they feel that you are there to listen to them and are their friend.

You need to be firm when applying safety rules, but find fun and interesting ways to deal with everyday chores such as brushing their teeth, getting dressed, putting their toys away, and even bedtime.

Just as you would with preschool kids, be sure to have the parents explain the rules and routine to you in front of the children. This way you can be sure that they know that their parents have told you everything!

COMMON CHARACTERISTICS OF SCHOOL-AGED CHILDREN
- very active
- the most independent age category, but will still need supervision
- have definite opinions
- have role models

Specific characteristics

5–6-year-olds
- very active
- hesitant to try new things and sometimes people-shy
- self-centred and think only about themselves

TIPS
• Talk to them in simple short sentences.
• Repeat important or safety information.
• Keep your play very visual.

6–8-year-olds
• have great imagination and are creative
• have lots of energy and may be active
• understand rules and consequences
• love to play in groups

TIPS
• can play alone, draw, or create without constant attention
• love stories—a great way to entertain them
• will like active play such as sports or playing with friends

8–10-year-olds
• have a clear understanding of the rules and consequences
• enjoy playing with friends
• have favourites and opinions on what they like

TIPS
• can play or do homework without constant attention
• can play more complex games
• are more independent and may resist assistance
• require supervision, although they may feel they don't need it

Feeding school-aged kids

If you are asked to feed the children a meal, try to include an activity that they can do safely while you are preparing the food. For example, they could colour or draw a picture at the kitchen table while you are preparing dinner. This is a good way to supervise them while you are busy.

Remember, always have children sit still while they are eating. If they are bouncing around, they could easily choke.

If it is left up to you to prepare dinner, think of some healthy foods that kids like. A sandwich and a glass of milk is usually a favourite for most kids. For snacks, crackers with jam or butter, milk, or fruit are good choices.

Bedtime for school-aged kids

School-aged children will also have definite routines for bedtime. Clarify the routines with the parents before they leave, and have them explain the bedtime routine to you in front of the children. This will ensure that the routine does not change when the parents are not there. Follow the bedtime routine, and you will have a much easier time putting preschoolers and school-aged children to bed.

Playtime for school-aged kids

School-aged children need to be supervised. It is a common belief that you don't have to watch older kids as much, but this is simply not true.

School-aged kids are more likely to have an accidental injury than toddlers and babies. This is usually because they are more active, like to show off to test their limits, and are not always constantly supervised.

A great babysitter knows that the best way to supervise children is to play with them and be involved in what they are doing.

If it is a nice day, a school-aged child may ride his bike, play sports outside, or play with neighbourhood friends. He certainly will want to run around and be active.

Make sure that you go with him everywhere. Even if a neighbour offers to include the child in a walk with his friend, you go along. Their parents hired you to babysit their child, not the neighbour. Besides, it is fun to watch kids communicate and play together. Be cautious of traffic and follow all bicycle safety rules, such as always wearing a helmet. Bring some games and activities with you that may be different from what the child has at home.

SAFE TOYS AND ACTIVITIES FOR SCHOOL-AGED CHILDREN
- sidewalk chalk
- markers
- paint
- construction paper
- building a fort with cardboard boxes or with pillows and blankets
- writing a play and acting it out
- doing an art show
- making a craft (come with ideas and supplies!)
- making a gift for their parents
- board games (examples: Monopoly, Operation, etc.)

Keeping things under control

Children have minds of their own, and sometimes getting them to listen to you may be difficult. You are in charge of their safety, and a great babysitter knows what is best as far as safety goes.

Babies and toddlers have no idea of the consequences of their actions. You may have to be firm if the toddler is doing something that might be unsafe. Try to distract her from the activity by offering her something fun and interesting and, of course, less dangerous.

Be specific and polite when you are asking the child to do something. For example, if you want the child to pick up her toys, say: "Pick up your toys that are on the floor, please."

Give the child warnings as well. For example, if you want the child to pick up her toys before naptime, ten minutes before naptime, say: "You have ten minutes before naptime. Please start picking up your toys that are on the floor." Then, five minutes before naptime, say: "You now have five minutes before naptime. Please pick up your toys that are on the floor." This will give the child the warning that playtime is ending and that she needs to clean up before naptime, and will give her some time to do so.

Whenever the child does something you like, tell her that you like what she did and why. Children love praise, and when you tell them what is a positive behaviour, they will know what types of behaviour you expect. Be consistent, too; don't change the rules! This will confuse the children because they won't know what you expect, and will create even more problems.

Remember at all times that you are the role model and the leader, and the children will look to you for guidance. You cannot expect them to follow the rules if you do not follow them yourself. Set a good example, and show them what a great babysitter you are!

Separation anxiety

Some children do not like to be away from their parents and may display signs of separation anxiety. They may cry and pull away from you, or become angry at their parents and you.

Be patient. Offer to play a favourite game or try to distract the child from his worries. Tell him that his parents will be back and that you are there to play games and hang out and have fun while they are gone. Reassure him that his parents will come home and that he will see them again.

Slowly he will begin to trust you, and you will experience less separation anxiety as time goes on.

Taking care of more than one child and age group

You may find that you are asked to babysit more than one child. You are ready to babysit more than one child if you and your parents feel that you have had enough experience and you can properly supervise them. Be sure to take extra time preparing for the task.

Two children usually means that you will have to think about two different age groups and their specific hazards and needs, and you will have to do this at the same time! It's not an easy task. So be sure that you can do it, and remember, a great babysitter always recognizes her limitations.

Be sure to talk to the parents ahead of time and get clear rules and guidelines. Let the kids in on the conversation.

Plan, plan, plan! Set out age-appropriate games and toys that both age groups can play with. Be cautious of toys that may be safe for older kids but not for the younger ones.

You may find that they will compete for your attention. Show them equal attention, and be sure to include both children in as many activities as you safely can.

Arguing with siblings

If you are babysitting more than one child and they are not getting along, you may find yourself in a difficult situation. Parents everywhere know what it is like to deal with brothers and sisters who are arguing. Talk to the parents and ask how they handle arguing or misbehaviour.

A great babysitter knows how to show equal attention to each child they are babysitting. If you are babysitting siblings who are fighting, find out what the problem is and try to settle it fairly. Stay calm and listen to their feelings.

If necessary, separate the siblings and give them each an equal time out. While they are separated, plan a fun activity that will take their minds off the original argument. Be sure that it involves both children equally.

Mark down the incident in your Report Card and be sure to let the parents know of the problem when they return. If you experience this repeatedly with the same clients, you may wish not to accept any further babysitting jobs. Remember, you always have the right to say no to any job offered.

If the arguing persists and you have exhausted your ideas for stopping it, call the parents. They may have an additional suggestion, or may talk to the children themselves. Remember, a babysitter never spanks, hits, or yells at a child, so these are not options for stopping the fighting.

A great babysitter knows what her abilities are and never takes on a responsibility without being prepared. You will soon find families and kids that you love to babysit for on a regular basis. Each child is different. A great babysitter takes the time to learn about the kids that she babysits and loves spending time with them, and it shows!

Problem Solving:

You are babysitting an 8-year-old boy and his 6-year-old sister. You have babysat for them in the past and know that they do not like to play together. The boy likes active games like road hockey and playing catch. The girl likes to sit and play with her dolls. What are some ideas for how you can share your time with both and supervise them at the same time?

_____

_____

_____

_____

_____

_____

_____

_____

_____

REVIEW QUESTIONS

1. What are some characteristics that are common to preschoolers (ages 3–5)?

a. very active, self-centred

b. boring and not interested in playing games

c. sleep a lot

2. What are some tips that you can use to help talk to this age group?

a. Talk in short simple sentences.

b. Keep play very visual.

c. Pay lots of attention to them.

d. all of the above

3. Babies' heads are very heavy. When picking up a baby, be sure to support the head and neck with your hands.

a. true

b. false

4. Never toss a baby in the air, even in play.

a. true

b. false

5. Babies can eat the same things as you do.

a. true

b. false

6. Warm the baby bottle in the microwave.

a. true

b. false

7. Circle all the safe places where you can put a baby while you are preparing food or a diaper change.

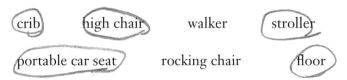

crib   high chair   walker   stroller

portable car seat   rocking chair   floor

8. How can you test to see if the formula or food is lukewarm?
a. Eat it.
b. Drop a bit on the inside of your wrist.
c. Give it to the baby.

9. It is important to burp babies...
a. before you feed them
b. after you feed them
c. never: Babies don't need to burp.

10. When putting a baby to sleep, it is okay to place him on his tummy.
a. true
b. false

11. When should you change a baby's diaper?
a. when it is soiled
b. every hour, regardless if it is soiled
c. after she wakes up from a nap

12. If you use a baby changing table, it is okay to leave the baby on the table while you get the diaper supplies together.
a. absolutely never
b. if there are rails

13. What kinds of toys are appropriate and safe for infants?
a. soft rubber teething toys
b. play activity gyms
c. small toys with many parts
d. a and b

14. When it is time to put the baby to sleep, it is best to
a. slow down the play and make the room very quiet
b. play very hard to tire him out
c. leave him in the crib alone until he falls asleep

15. What is the best way to supervise toddlers?
a. Follow them around.
b. Restrict their toys and movement.
c. Don't let them play with dangerous things.
d. Play with them.

16. How old is a toddler?
a. 3–5 years old
b. 1–3 years old
c. 5–8 years old

17. Name an age-appropriate toy for a toddler.
Teddy bear

18. If you are babysitting two children and they begin to argue, the best way to deal with them is to
a. ignore them until they eventually stop arguing
b. find out what the problem is and look for a positive, fair resolution
c. separate them and don't let them talk again until their parents get home

19. DEFINITIONS

Please put the correct answer in the box provided.

☐ cradle

☐ formula

☐ lukewarm

☐ bottle nipple

☐ colicky

☐ diaper rash

☐ baby monitor

☐ friction

☐ allergies

Answers:

a. a liquid food for infants containing most of the nutrients in human milk

b. moderately warm; not hot; tepid

c. the rubber cap on a bottle from which a baby nurses

d. suffering from excessive gas

e. an electronic device used to transmit sounds when you are not in the room

f. the rubbing of one object or surface against another

g. an abnormally high sensitivity to certain substances, such as pollens, foods

h. soreness and redness on the skin of the thighs and buttocks of infants

i. a baby bed with sides and rockers

FOUR

Safety

Preventing injury

The most important thing great babysitters can do is to keep the kids that they are caring for safe while their parents are away. We can't stress enough how important this is to both the parents and the kids.

Kidproof Safety's main goal is to increase safety awareness, and we take that very seriously. We believe in taking preventive and proactive measures, which means being aware of hazards and avoiding dangerous situations. This section is dedicated to making sure that you know how to make safe choices, and if an emergency situation does occur, that you are prepared and know what to do.

It is important to point out that it is the responsibility of the parents to provide a safe home for you and their kids. However, not everyone may be as safety-conscious as they should be. Many accidents are caused by people not taking the precautions they should. Keeping a safe home and play area is not as difficult as you may think.

Identifying hazards

Great babysitters know the limits of their abilities and environment and how to safely supervise children of all ages.

It is not difficult to make safe choices and to see the warning signs. But it is very easy to ignore them. Now is a great time to start to develop your safety senses and sharpen your observation skills to look beyond what you see in front of you. Train your mind to question things that seem unusual, and trust your instincts. A great babysitter is a mini-expert in predicting danger.

If this is your first time babysitting for a client, request that they walk you through the house, and take special note of possible safety concerns. Go through your Safety Checklist with the parents. This is a great time to ask any questions that may have come up. Some parents might just take it for granted that you know where certain items are. Don't be afraid to ask where the fire extinguisher is and if there is an alarm in the house.

Be sure to ask if there are any rooms that are off limits to the kids and to you. Respect their rules.

Take a close look at the home that you are working in. Make a mental note of where the safety devices are and, more important, where they are not.

If you are babysitting small children, be sure to get down on your knees and take a look at each room that the kids will be in so you can see what is eye level to them. This is an entirely different perspective, and you may see dangers that you could not see from your height. This is also a great icebreaking activity to do with the children whom you are babysitting and doubles as a quick lesson on home safety for them.

> **TIP**
> The key to being safe is being able to look ahead, pay attention to the warning signs, and act on them before an accident happens.

Have the children point out if they see anything that may be dangerous for them. If you identify things, make a note on the Report Card, remove them if you can, or pay close attention to them if you can't. The key is to identify dangers ahead of time.

What to look for

The following are the different types of hazards and the sources of these hazards:

POISON HAZARDS

Sources

- cleaners
- paint
- medicines and vitamins
- plants

Prevention

- Make sure the poison hazards are in locked cabinets.

- If the cabinets are not locked, make sure the children stay away from them.

- Lock cabinets.

- Shut all bathroom and extra bedroom doors.

- Shut and lock the door leading to the garage.

WATER HAZARDS

Sources

- pools
- toilets
- bathtubs filled with water
- fish tanks
- ponds
- fountains

Prevention

- Supervise children at all times, especially when they are around any water.

- If there is a fence around the pool, make sure the gate is closed.

- If it is necessary for a young child to have a bath, supervise him.

- Be aware of any water hazards and block access to them.

Don't forget about the toilet bowl! Toddlers are top-heavy and an open toilet can be one of the most dangerous places. Water is fun to play with, and toddlers have been known to reach into toilet bowls and fall in headfirst. They will not have the strength to pull themselves out and could easily drown. Be sure to close all bathroom doors.

CHOKING HAZARDS

Sources

- small objects such as marbles, buttons, paper clips
- balloons
- pillows and blankets can be choking and suffocation hazards for babies who are not able to sit up

There are many choking hazards for children under three years of age. They include, but are not limited to
- string or yarn
- popcorn
- plastic bags
- rubber bands
- small toys and parts
- whole hot dogs

A great way to find out if an item may be a choking hazard is to use the toilet-roll test. Any object that can fit through a toilet-roll cardboard tube is too small for a child under three years of age and is a choking hazard.

Prevention

- Remove all choking hazards from the rooms that you and the children will be in.

- Block access to any rooms that choking hazards remain in.

- If you are unsure if an object is safe or not, remove it—it is better to be on the safe side.

INJURY HAZARDS

Sources

- sharp and pointed objects (Watch sharp table corners with toddlers!)
- toys with small parts
- stairs
- scissors
- pins and needles
- ladders
- bicycles and tricycles
- skateboards and in-line skates
- baseball bats

Prevention

- Remove all injury hazards from the rooms that you and the children will be in.

- Block access to any rooms that injury hazards remain in.

- Use safety gates on stairs.

- Use safety rails on cribs.

- If children are riding their bicycles, make sure they wear their helmets

- If children are using in-line skates, make sure they wear a helmet, elbow and knee pads, and wrist guards.

BITE AND STING HAZARDS

Sources

- bees and wasps
- fire ants
- spiders
- snakes
- dogs and cats (even family pets!)

Prevention

- Be aware of any allergies the children have to stings (and what to do if they have an allergy and are stung).

- Keep children away from other people's pets, or any animals they don't know.

- Remind children to be careful around their own pets as well, and do not leave them alone with them.

- Keep children out of areas where stings could occur.

BURN HAZARDS

Sources

- hot foods or liquids
- the sun
- electrical outlets
- ovens and grills

Prevention

- Test the temperature of food yourself before giving it to the children.

- Don't microwave water, and remember that foods that are cooked in the microwave can be cool on the outside but hot (very hot!) on the inside.

- Don't eat or drink anything hot when you are holding a baby or toddler.

- Don't pick up anything hot without using oven mitts.

- Keep children away from the stove, or anything hot.

- When children are outside playing, make sure they have sunscreen on.

FIRE HAZARDS

Sources

- fireplace
- stove
- firepit
- matches
- lighter

Prevention

- Do not let children play with matches or lighters; remove them and place them in a spot that is out of the children's reach.

- Do not use matches or a lighter.

- Block access to fireplaces and any outdoor firepits.

- Do not light any fires in the fireplace or outdoor firepit.

- Make sure you know where the fire extinguisher is, and that the smoke alarms are working.

ENVIRONMENTAL HAZARDS

Here is a list of items that are commonly used to baby-proof a house. Be sure to go through your Safety Checklist each time you babysit. That way, you will have a better understanding of how childproof your environment really is.

Be sure to check for
• locks on cupboard doors
• electrical outlet covers
• door guards

Do you have any other suggestions?

_____

_____

_____

These are terrific additions to ensure a safe home, but a great babysitter knows that she still needs to supervise the children, even with safety products present.

Most commercial child products such as cribs, strollers, and high chairs must endure some very strict safety testing and follow guidelines before they can even be sold.

But this does not mean that people do not still use items that have not been rigorously tested. Some parents use the same crib that they had as a baby and are not aware of the hazards.

Carefully check to be sure that you know the equipment that you are being provided with to do the job is safe, not just for the children that you babysit, but also for yourself. Many young

Are you a great babysitter?

To be a great babysitter you have to be prepared for any situation. Think you're up to the challenge? Use this worksheet to find out. If you don't know all the answers, don't worry. You can find them in *The Babysitter's Handbook*.

Name two safe ways to get a babysitting job.
a. Advertise in a library that you are available to babysit.
b. Tell younger kids you know that you are available to babysit.
c. Answer an ad in the paper.
d. Tell relatives and family friends that you are available to babysit.

Babies can eat the same things as you do.
a. true
b. false

What are some characteristics that are common to preschoolers (ages 3–5 years)?
a. very active, self centred
b. boring and not interested in playing games
c. sleep a lot

What is the best way to supervise toddlers?
a. Follow them around.
b. Restrict their toys and movement.
c. Don't let them play with dangerous things.
d. Play with them.

If there is a fire in the house you should
a. immediately get the children out of the house and call 911 from the neighbours'
b. throw a blanket over it
c. hide upstairs with the kids
d. go back into the house and get the pets

SAMANTHA WILSON   author of SAFE KIDS, SAFE FAMILIES
& THE BABYSITTER'S HANDBOOK

Be a Hazard Detective

Can you describe the hazards?

Parents can also help you become a great babysitter. When taking a new job, remind parents of the type of information you need to know to keep their children safe and happy. Here are some questions you can ask:

- Will I be preparing snacks or meals?

- Do your children have any allergies or take any medications?

- Do you have a fire escape plan?

- What's your neighbour's name and phone number?

- How would you like me to handle misbehaviour?

- What is your children's bedtime routine?

- Is there a pet door or do I need to let the pet out?

- Do I need to put sunscreen lotion or insect repellent on your children when they play outside?

- What are your children's favourite games?

SAMANTHA WILSON author of SAFE KIDS, SAFE FAMILIES
& THE BABYSITTER'S HANDBOOK

people are injured on the job. This can include babysitters, so watch out for yourself as well as the kids you are looking after.

The best way to prevent dangerous situations from occurring is to supervise children at all times.

It is the employer's obligation to provide a safe work environment for you. Make sure that you are comfortable and confident in your position. If you do not feel safe, do not take the job. Be sure to fill out the Safety Checklist.

Strangers, phone calls, and unexpected visitors

Great babysitters always look ahead to predict possible threats or dangers for both themselves and the kids they are babysitting. The first thing a great babysitter does when the parents leave is lock all the doors and windows of the house, even during the daytime.

If you are not expecting anyone, do not open the door or even answer it by talking through the locked door. Most doors have windows or peepholes so that you can have a look at who is at the door. Remember that if it is very important they will come back when the clients are home.

Make a note on the Report Card that someone came to the door.

If someone is at the door and is not going away, call your parents or another adult whom you trust to come to the house. If it is an emergency—if an intruder is trying to break into the house—call 911.

Answering the telephone has the same rule. Do not answer the phone if you don't know who is calling.

Many phones now have caller ID. This is where the name and phone number of the person calling shows up on the screen of the phone. If the telephone rings, first check to see if you recognize the caller through caller ID. Only answer it if you know who is calling.

If the phone does not have caller ID, you will not be able to tell who is calling. It could be your parents or the client calling to see how you are all doing. We suggest that you set up a phone code ring that will help you identify the caller before you pick up the receiver.

For example, agree with your parents that if they call you, they will hang up after the first ring, then immediately call back. If you hear the code ring first, it is likely that the next caller will be your parents, and you may pick it up. Arrange a code ring with your client as well.

You should also arrange ahead of time what time you can expect their call. This way you can be prepared to listen for the code ring at a specific time.

If you and the children are playing outside and someone you don't know asks to use the phone or toilet, simply tell them no. You don't need to give them an explanation. They will move on. If the stranger does not leave, take the kids into the house and lock the door behind you. Never let anyone into the house while you are Babysitting. Be sure to make a note of the incident on your Report Card.

Fire safety

When you are going through the house with the parents before they leave, be sure to ask them to show you where the fire extinguishers are located. Make a mental note whether there are smoke alarms and carbon monoxide detectors on each floor.

Also ask the parents if they have an escape plan in the case of a fire, and if the kids are aware of it and have practised it. Ask them to explain it to you before they go, and be sure you fully understand the route before they leave. Know two exits from each room, and be sure to note rooms with only one exit. If the house has two storeys, ask the parents how you can escape from upstairs. Make note of this on your Safety Checklist.

What to do if there is a fire!

Fire spreads very fast. If there is a fire, follow these steps:

1. Get everyone out of the house first and don't stop for any personal items or pets. If there is smoke, get down on your knees and crawl (smoke rises, so you need to get as close to the floor as possible, where the air is cleaner).

2. Have a meeting place outside of the house. This is where everyone will go once they are outside. Count heads to make sure all the children are there.

3. Run to a neighbour's house and call 911.

4. If you can't get past the fire, close the doors between you and the fire. Be sure to touch the door before opening it. If it is hot, do not open it. Call for help.

5. If your clothing is on fire, STOP, DROP, AND ROLL. Stop immediately, drop to the floor and cover your face with your hands, and roll on the floor. Keep rolling until the fire is out. Do not run. If a child's clothing is on fire, smother the flames with a blanket or a jacket while the child is on the ground.

6. Wait outside for the fire department to arrive. Tell them if there is a pet inside the house.

Never go back into the house.

Emergencies and EMS

EMS stands for Emergency Medical Services. This can include the police, ambulance, and fire departments.

Most cities and towns have a full EMS service. When you dial 911, you will get all three services. However, some smaller rural towns still do not have 911 service. Instead they have a full telephone number that you have to dial to reach the EMS.

Be sure to find out if the area you live and babysit in has the 911 service. If it doesn't, get the alternate number and put it on your Emergency Phone List sheet.

When to call EMS

A person calls EMS when there is an emergency situation that requires the help of a police officer, paramedic, or fire-fighter. For example, you would call EMS to report a fire, a break-in or attempted break-in, for an ambulance, or in any situation where someone could be or has been seriously injured or killed.

Calling EMS: what to say

When you call EMS, it is very important to stay calm. There are a number of questions the operator will ask you, and it is very important that they get the information from you. Remember, they are relying on you to tell them what the problem is and how they can help!

When you call EMS, you will need to know information such as the following:

1. **Location:** They will want to know where the emergency situation is happening. You will need to tell them the street address, house or apartment number, and the phone number.

2. **Type of emergency:** They will want to know the type of emergency. For example, whether it is a fire, break-in, medical, or other type of emergency.

3. **Injuries:** They will need to know if there are any injuries and, if so, how they occurred. They will ask you if the victim is breathing.

4. **Medications:** They will need to know if the victim is on any medications. You should have this written on your Emergency Phone List.

5. **Age:** They will need to know the age of the victim.

6. **Do not hang up** until the EMS operator tells you to. Stay on the line.

The operator will likely stay on the line with you until help arrives. Let them know when the ambulance, police, or fire department has arrived. You will need to let them in, and they may ask you some questions as well, so be prepared with your information again.

Arriving home safely

A great babysitter knows how to take good care of the client's children, but also knows how to take care of herself. This includes making sure that you arrive home safely from the job.

When you agree to accept a babysitting job, ask how you will get home. Ask the client if they will give you a ride home, and if the answer is no, make sure to check with your parents that they can pick you up—before you agree to take the job.

If the client has agreed to take you home and you feel uncomfortable because you feel they have had too much to drink, or for any other reason, politely refuse the ride. Call your parents and ask them to come and get you. If you feel uncomfortable telling the client that you do not want them to drive you home, have a code set up with your parents.

For example, pre-arrange with your parents that if you call them and say, "I am on my way home now," this means that you want them to come and pick you up. Once you are off the phone, you can tell the client that your parents were confused about who was taking you home, so they are on their way to come and get you. It will be too late to call them back because they are on their way. This way you arrive home safely and you can avoid having to explain to the client why you don't want them to take you home.

Practise!

The best away to prepare for any emergency is to role-play what to do. When you role-play an event in your mind, your brain will have something to use to help you make safe choices if you are faced with a similar event in the future. This is how professional EMS workers train to handle all types of emergencies.

Problem Solving:
Fire

You are sitting in the playroom downstairs playing a game with five-year-old Bobby. His sister, Sarah, is upstairs sleeping. Suddenly you smell smoke coming from the kitchen.
What do you do?

_____

_____

_____

_____

_____

_____

_____

_____

Power outage

You are babysitting in the winter. There is a very bad storm. It is dark, but still early, and both Bobby and Sarah are awake and watching cartoons in the family room. Suddenly the power goes out. What do you do?

_____

_____

_____

_____

_____

Parents are late or delayed

You are babysitting Bobby and Sarah on a Saturday night. You agreed to babysit only until midnight because you have a soccer game early the next morning. You get a phone call from the parents at 11:30 p.m. They tell you that they will be late and won't be home for a couple more hours. Bobby and Sarah are sleeping. What do you do?

_____

_____

_____

_____

_____

NOTES

_____

_____

_____

_____

_____

_____

_____

_____

_____

_____

_____

_____

_____

_____

_____

SAFETY

SAFETY

REVIEW QUESTIONS

1. The key to being safe is:

a. Look ahead, pay attention to the warning signs, and act before an accident happens.

b. Cross your fingers and hope that nothing happens.

c. You don't have to worry about it because it is the responsibility of the parents to make sure that everything is safe.

2. The first time that you babysit for a new client you must

a. ask them to walk you through the house to make note of any safety hazards

b. ask where the fire extinguisher is

c. ask how the doors and windows lock

d. all of the above

3. If you see items that may be unsafe you should

a. tell the parent that you will not babysit until they fix them

b. remove them or make note and be extra cautious

c. ignore them. If the family lives with it, so can you.

4. What is the best way to see what hazards a toddler faces in the house?

a. Get down on your hands and knees and look at the room from their angle.

b. Ask them.

c. Don't worry; the parents will have taken care of all hazards.

5. If someone you are not expecting comes to the door while you are babysitting, you should:

a. answer it and tell them that you are the babysitter and the parents will be home later

b. talk through the door and tell the person that you can't open the door

c. not answer the door. Make a note of it on your Report Card.

6. If the phone rings you should

a. not answer it unless it is a code ring or call display tells you who the caller is. Note it on the Report Card.
b. answer it and say that the parent is in the shower
c. answer it and tell them that the parents are home and offer to take a message

7. If there is a fire in the house you should

a. immediately get the children out of the house and call 911 from a neighbour's
b. throw a blanket over it
c. hide upstairs with the kids
d. go back into the house and get the pets

8. What does EMS stand for?

a. Emergency Medical Services
b. Everyone's Medical Services
c. Emergency Monitored System

9. What services do you get if you call 911?

a. the police
b. the fire department
c. an ambulance
d. all three

10. What is the best way to practise what to do in an emergency?

a. Role-play realistic events.
b. Remember what you saw EMS do on TV.
c. Wait until something happens and react the best you can.

11. DEFINITIONS

Please put the correct answer in the box provided.

☐ Carbon monoxide

☐ Fire escape plan

Answers:
a. a planned escape route from different parts of a house, used in case of a fire
b. a colourless, odourless highly poisonous gas

NOTES

_____

_____

_____

_____

_____

_____

_____

_____

_____

_____

_____

_____

_____

_____

_____

_____

SAFETY

FIVE

Abuse, Neglect, and Protecting Kids

If you want to babysit, it is obvious that you love kids and want to take care of them. Great babysitters will find that the kids they babysit will soon trust them and, at times, confide in them.

Most kids just want to be loved and cared for, and they deserve to have all the love and support possible. Unfortunately, some children live in homes that are not safe and are raised by adults who do not always look out for them or protect them as well as they should. As a great babysitter, you may find yourself caring for children who live in dangerous environments.

First, it is important to understand that you can make a difference in a child's life. You have the ability and the obligation to tell someone if you think a child that you are caring for, or even a friend, is being abused or neglected.

Child abuse is when a child is being hurt physically, emotionally, or sexually. They may show signs of abuse such as bruises, burns, bite marks, or recent scars.

Children who are being physically abused may act out in anger, become very aggressive, or make excuses as they try to hide their bruises or injuries. They may not like physical attention and shy away quite easily.

TIP
Great babysitters not only know how to talk to kids, they also know how to listen.

PROTECTING KIDS

A child who is being sexually abused may act out in a very sexual way. You may see signs of injuries to their genitals while changing their diapers or dressing them, or they may not want to be physically touched.

Child neglect is a bit harder to determine. Just because a house is very untidy does not necessarily mean that the children are being neglected. On the other hand, a neglected child may always seem to be hungry, tired, or scared, or cry easily. He may also act out the opposite way and become very aggressive and difficult. A neglected child does not have proper food, clothing, or shelter, and is not being cared for by the parents.

It can be frightening to think about, but great babysitters always look out for kids and care about everyone in their surroundings. If you feel that someone is being hurt, you must go to an adult whom you trust and tell them how you feel and why you feel this way.

If this adult dismisses your concerns, tell another one. Keep telling until someone listens and takes your concerns further. Don't worry about being wrong; it is not your job to investigate the situation—leave that up to the professionals. It is your job to report it and watch out for other kids.

Appropriate and inappropriate touching

If at any time the children you babysit, someone you know, or anyone else tells you that an adult has touched them or asked them to touch the adult in their private areas (the places a bathing suit covers), you must immediately tell an adult whom you trust.

It is very important to understand that you are actually help-ing the children by reporting possible sexual abuse, and not breaking their trust. If the adult dismisses your concerns, tell another and another until someone calls the police.

Can you think of three people whom you trust to listen to your concerns?

Write them down.

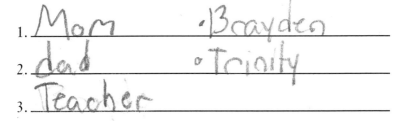

1. Mom ·Brayden
2. dad ·Trinity
3. Teacher

If an adult touches you inappropriately or talks about things that make you feel uncomfortable, it is very important that you listen to your instincts and do not continue to babysit for them. Immediately tell an adult you trust and do not babysit for that person again. Remember, you have the right to refuse any job offer.

If you feel that a child you are babysitting or know is being neglected or physically or sexually abused:

1. Tell an adult you trust and keep telling until someone calls the police or other helping agencies.

2. Don't confront the child or the parents. This could make the situation worse.

3. If a child you are babysitting tells you that he is being abused, immediately call an adult you trust and they will call the police.

NOTES

_____

_____

_____

_____

_____

_____

_____

_____

_____

_____

_____

_____

_____

_____

_____

REVIEW QUESTIONS

1. If you think that a child you are babysitting or a friend is being abused or neglected, you should
a. talk to them and find out if it is true
b. tell an adult you trust and discuss what to do
c. ignore it. It is none of your business.

2. If a child you are babysitting tells you that an adult has been touching them in their private areas (the places a bathing suit covers), you should
a. confront the adult
b. tell an adult you trust immediately
c. investigate further before talking to an adult
d. ignore it. The child may be lying and you don't want to cause any problems.

3. If someone you are babysitting for makes sexual comments or advances that make you uncomfortable, you should
a. refuse to babysit for them again
b. tell an adult you trust
c. all of the above

4. Child abuse is when a child is being hurt either physically, emotionally, or sexually
a. true
b. false

5. Child neglect is when someone does not take proper care of a child.
a. true
b. false

NOTES

SIX
Babysitter's First Aid

A great babysitter knows her limitations and abilities. Babysitting is serious business. You will be responsible for the safety of the children left in your care.

We have already learned how to look ahead and predict dangerous situations and prevent accidents that may cause injuries. Good job. But accidents still happen, even to great babysitters. So it is important that you are prepared to safely respond to an emergency in a calm, rational, and skilled manner.

First, this is not a certified first aid course. If you like, you can choose to take a first aid and certified CPR program later, to build on the skills that we are going to discuss. In fact, we recommend it.

For now, though, let's concentrate on understanding what an emergency is and learn the approach to handling an emergency in a safe and timely manner.

An emergency is when a serious situation or occurrence happens unexpectedly and demands immediate action.

Some examples of a medical emergency are:

• Someone is not breathing.

• Someone is unconscious.

• Someone is bleeding very badly.

• Someone has been poisoned.

Some examples of non-medical emergencies are:

• Someone is trying to break into the house.

• Someone is hitting you or beating you up.

• A fire has broken out in the house.

If you feel that an emergency is happening, call 911. If you can, direct someone else to call for you so that you can stay with the injured person.

First aid

Although great babysitters provide excellent and constant supervision, accidents may still happen. Almost all injuries can be prevented. You need to take the time to complete your Safety Checklist and ask the parents questions that will help you not only care for the children, but also provide a safer environment for them.

If an accident occurs, no matter how minor, you must write it down in detail on the Report Card, and always tell the parents on their return. If it is a major accident or injury, you should contact them at the emergency number that they have provided.

Do not be concerned about what the parents will think of your skills; the safety of the child you are babysitting is your first priority. In order for parents to administer ongoing first aid, they will need a full and accurate account of the injuries.

We hope that you will never need to use the skills on the following pages, but you need to realize the importance of understanding them. Remember, these are guidelines and do not replace the advice of a doctor or emergency professional. They are guidelines based on common and accepted first aid practices.

We recommend that you enroll in a certified first aid program to learn advanced skills and CPR to be better prepared for any emergency.

Choking and breathing difficulties

A great babysitter has taken the time to learn about the children he is caring for. This includes understanding any allergies, medical conditions, and choking hazards that may be present in the home.

If you find something that you consider to be a choking hazard, immediately remove it and place it safely away from the child. Don't bring any snacks with you that may cause an allergic reaction, and supervision at all times will help assure that the children are well cared for.

The most common reasons for a child to suddenly encounter breathing difficulties are allergies, asthma, and choking.

It is vital that you understand what to do in each of these emergency situations. Remember to always stay calm.

Allergies

Some children are allergic to food and other things, which can be potentially life-threatening if not treated immediately. Some common items are shellfish, nuts, medicine, and insect bites. During your initial interview, be sure to ask if the child has any allergies. If so, ask if they are severe, and what is the treatment for them. It is best to stick with what has worked for the parents in the past and follow their advice. Don't bring any snacks with you that may cause an allergic reaction. Some children are so allergic to specific things that the smell alone can cause symptoms.

Anaphylactic shock

You may have heard this term before. This is a type of reaction from allergic exposure. It can be caused by insect bites or stings, nuts, or other food allergies. It usually begins within minutes of exposure to the substance causing the allergy. The airways will narrow and make it very difficult to breathe. Within 15 minutes, anaphylactic shock can kill a person if it is not treated.

Some signs of anaphylactic shock:

• difficulty breathing (noisy or wheezy)

• swollen tongue, eyes, or face

• pounding heart

• difficulty swallowing

• dizziness, weakness

• unconsciousness

Treatment

If you suspect that a child is in anaphylactic shock, immediately call 911. You may follow the procedures that the parents have demonstrated and provided. Make sure that the item that caused the allergic reaction is removed. Comfort the child and monitor her breathing until EMS arrives.

Asthma

Many children suffer from asthma. This is a disease that affects the airways, which are the tubes that carry air in and out of your lungs. If you have asthma, the insides of your airways become swollen. The inflammation makes the airways very sensitive, and they will react to irritants by narrowing and letting less air flow into the lungs.

Some symptoms of asthma are a whistling or wheezing sound when breathing. Other symptoms include coughing, chest tightness, and trouble breathing. For most children asthma is controlled through inhalers and other medications. If you are babysitting a child with asthma, be sure that you clearly understand the treatment and limits that you will need to follow.

Choking

Choking can be a hazard for most kids, especially if you are babysitting two or more children who are several years apart. This is because one child may be old enough to safely play with small toys and another may not. These small toys and items can be a serious safety hazard for small children. When you are completing your safety check, be sure to note the toys and items that you feel may be dangerous. If you find something that you would consider to be a choking hazard, immediately remove it and place it safely away from the child.

If the child puts a small object or food in his mouth and it becomes lodged, blocking his airway, you will need to respond quickly.

TIP
Some signs that children may be choking are: holding their throat with their hand, turning blue in the face, coughing.

Partial blockage

This is when an item is only partially blocking the child's airway. Air, although minimal, may be getting through. The child will start to cough and appear distressed. Stay with the child and encourage him to sit still and continue to cough. The item may dislodge itself.

Do not pat the child on the back. You could cause the blockage to become completely lodged and prevent breathing all together.

TIP
If the child can make a noise, he has only a partial blockage.

Complete blockage

If a partial blockage suddenly becomes a complete blockage, you will need to react quickly. This means that no air is passing through. The child will not be able to cough or make any sound at all. He will quickly turn blue in the face if the blockage is not cleared.

If the child has a complete blockage, you must react immediately. Call 911, then begin to perform abdominal thrusts.

Abdominal thrusts

For children over 1 year old
Stand behind the child and place your arms around his waist. Make a fist with one hand and press it just above his belly button. Wrap your other arm around his waist and hold onto your hand. It should feel like you are hugging him from behind. Move your fists in and up tightly in the shape of the letter J. Think of it as a bear hug.

Continue this motion with as much force as necessary to dislodge the obstruction from the airway or until EMS arrives.

Infant (under 1 year old)
We do not recommend that anyone (adult or youth) babysit an infant without current certified first aid training. If you are caring for an infant who is under a year old, you must consider taking a certified first aid course to build confidence and the skills required to perform rescue breathing if necessary. Check your local hospital or first aid provider for a class near you before considering caring for an infant unsupervised.

Prevention

• Keep small objects a child could choke on out of reach and do not give gum (especially bubble gum), nuts, hard candy, or popcorn to children under 5 years old.

• Lock up all medications and poisonous substances so small children can't get to them.

- Don't let the children play while they are eating.

- Cut food into small chewable pieces.

- Avoid food that can cause choking, such as carrots, grapes, hot dogs, and large pieces of meat.

Cuts, scrapes, and punctures

Playing hard is part of being a kid. And part of being a great babysitter is accepting that there may come a time when the child you are caring for becomes injured. If you are supervising properly, an accident will result in just a slight scrape or scratch.

Nevertheless, for a small child, a boo-boo can be devastating. Be sure to understand that many kids need reassurance that you are there to take care of them, even if it is a minor mishap. Sometimes a hug is all that is needed.

Let's first determine the difference between cuts, scrapes, and punctures. You can treat most of these injuries yourself, although some may need extra attention.

Cuts

Cuts are injuries that slice the skin open. They can bleed only a little bit, or quite heavily. If the bleeding is very heavy and does not stop with simple pressure and rest, you should call 911. Some cuts are deep enough that they require immediate medical attention to stitch or glue them shut.

Scrapes

Scrapes tend to hurt only the top part of your skin. They can certainly sting more than a cut, but they will also heal a lot faster. You can treat a scrape with antiseptic wipes (to keep it clean), a Band-Aid, and, of course, some cuddles!

Punctures

Punctures are injuries that stab into the skin. They can be minor or major, deep stabs. Great babysitters should not encounter a puncture injury if they are properly supervising the children. Deep puncture wounds will require immediate medical attention.

Treatment for cuts and scrapes

1. Clean around the wound with water.

2. Use a sterile bandage or clean cloth and apply pressure on the cut to stop the bleeding. Do not put pressure on if there is glass or another object in the cut.

3. Continue applying pressure for up to 10 minutes if you need to. Use a sterile bandage or a clean cloth. You should have these items in your babysitter's kit. (Try not to use dry gauze. It can stick to the wound.)

4. Hold the injury higher than the heart. This slows down blood flow to that spot.

5. Put one or more Band-Aids on the cut. Do it this way:

- Put the Band-Aid across the cut so it can help hold the cut together.

- The sides of the cut skin should touch but not overlap.

- Don't touch the cut with your fingers.

- You can use a butterfly bandage if you have one.

- Use more than one bandage for a long cut.

- For scrapes, make a bandage from gauze and first-aid tape.

If the cut is still bleeding after 20 minutes, you should call 911. Keep pressure on the wound while you wait for help.

Be sure to advise the parents of the injury and the reasons for it as soon as they return. Remember, accidents happen. It is how you respond to them that can make all the difference in the world. Be honest, tell the parents exactly what happened and what you felt went wrong. They will appreciate your honesty and confirm that you are a true professional.

Nosebleeds

Nosebleeds are a common part of childhood. Most nosebleeds are caused from broken blood vessels just inside the front of the nose. Some causes for nosebleeds may be

- blowing your nose very hard or coughing

- nose-picking

- a cold

- allergies

- very cold or very dry air

- a punch or hit to the nose

Blood usually only comes out of one nostril. You should be able to treat this kind of nosebleed easily. Often the bleeding will stop on its own.

Treatment

The following procedure is recommended to treat minor nosebleeds:

Sit the child down, have her lean forward, and place a Kleenex or sterile cloth on the nose. Pinch the nostrils shut by using your thumb and forefinger to gently squeeze for 15 uninterrupted minutes. Tell the child to breathe through her mouth and continue to hold the cloth until the bleeding slows to a stop. This may take up to 15 minutes, so be patient.

Once the bleeding stops, make sure that the child does not blow her nose for at least 24 hours. Choose a quiet play activity. Be sure to make a note of the incident on your Report Card.

If the nose is bleeding very heavily or is a result of a fall or head injury, call 911.

Head injuries

One of the most common injuries that are treated in hospitals are related to children falling. Be sure to keep constant supervision on the children you are hired to care for. Remember that small children love to climb. If you make sure that their playtime is safe, head injuries should not be a concern.

A head injury can cause bleeding on the brain many hours after the injury. If the child has fallen you must advise the parents. Even if he appears to be fine, parents need to know of the incident so that they can keep a close eye on symptoms over the next 24 hours. Bleeding in the brain often starts within the first 24 hours after a head injury and can last for three days or longer.

Signs and symptoms of head injuries that must have medical attention:

• unconsciousness, confusion, or drowsiness

• inability to move a part of the body or weakness in an arm or leg

• a dent, bruise, cut, or blood on the scalp

• severe headache

• stiff neck

• vomiting

• blood or fluid that comes from the mouth, nose, or ears

• loss of vision, blurred or double vision, pupils of unequal size

• convulsions

Burns

Remember that most injuries are preventable. Burns are no exception. A great babysitter is not only prepared, but also conscious of dangers both inside and outside the home. Let's see what are the most common types of burns, how they are caused, how to treat them, and, most important, how to prevent them.

Burns can result from fire (dry heat), steam, boiling water (moist heat), chemicals (acid), and sunlight (sunburn).

Each type of burn can vary in severity. The severity is based on how deep the burn is (how many layers of skin are burnt), how much of the body is burnt, and where the burn is on the body. Most burns fall within three categories.

First-degree burns

These affect only the outer layer of your skin. The burnt area can be dry, red, and slightly swollen. A first-degree burn is painful and sensitive to touch. A mild sunburn and brief contact with a heat source such as a curling iron are good examples of first-degree burns. A first-degree burn should heal in about a week if there are no other problems.

Treatment

Apply a cool cloth or water to the affected area.

Second-degree burns

These more serious burns affect the skin's lower layers as well as the outer skin. They are painful and swollen, and show redness and blisters. The skin also develops a watery surface. Examples of second-degree burns are severe sunburn and boiling water burns.

First-aid procedures can be used to treat many second-degree burns, depending on their location and how much area is affected. These burns can be extremely painful.

Treatment

Cool the burned area for 10–30 minutes with either cold running water or a wet, cold compress. If the arm(s) or leg(s) are burned, elevate them above heart level. Cover the burned area with a clear cloth or sterile dressing. Don't use plastic.

Third-degree burns

These are the most serious burns, affecting both the outer and deep layers of the skin. They can also affect the underlying tissue and organs. They appear black-and-white and charred. The skin is swollen and underlying tissue is often exposed. Third-degree burns may not be as painful as first- or seconddegree burns. In fact, if the burn has destroyed the nerve endings, there may be no pain at all.

Third-degree burns can be caused by fire, burning clothing, or electric shocks. They always require emergency treatment and often result in hospitalization.

Prevention of burns

Supervision and preparation are the keys to preventing burns. Some safe practices are to not use the stove or light fires and to keep all matches and lighters safely away from children. You should identify possible burn hazards during your safety check at the start of the babysitting job.

BABYSITTER'S FIRST AID

Remember, if any injuries, even minor ones, occur, you must tell the parents.

Poisons

A child can be poisoned by inhaling, swallowing, or touching a poisonous substance. Prevention is the best protection against accidental poisoning. Be sure to look for potential poison hazards as you complete the Safety Checklist. Remove all hazards from a child's reach. Be sure to advise the parents upon their return where you placed the items.

Make sure that you have your local poison control centre telephone number within reach. It should be on your emergency contact list. You can find your local number in the front pages of the phone book.

Although many products will list what to do in case of accidental poisoning, you should still call Poison Control for instructions. If you know the cause of the poisoning, give the poison control centre as much information as you can. This information includes the name and make of the product, if the product was swallowed, inhaled, or came in contact with skin, how much of the product was taken, and details such as the age and symptoms of the child.

Follow the instructions given to you by the poison control centre. You may have to call 911.

Prevention of poisoning

Keep all poisonous substances such as household products, medicines, and plants out of children's reach, preferably behind locked doors or too high for them to reach even when climbing on a chair or counter.

Always read warning labels on pesticides, household cleaners, and other products that could be poisonous. Follow instructions for use and storage.

A great babysitter knows how important it is to stay calm in an emergency. If you suspect that the child you are caring for has been poisoned, do not panic. You need to act quickly.

If the child is conscious, call the poison control centre immediately. Try to determine the cause of the poisoning. If the child inhaled a poison, remove him from the toxic air.

If the child is unconscious, you must immediately call 911. If the child is not breathing you may need to perform artificial respiration as you learned it in a certified first-aid and CPR program.

Certified first-aid and CPR training

Great babysitters are committed to keeping their skills sharp. The Babysitter's First Aid component is a great introduction to basic first-aid skills. We also recommend that you enroll in a certified first-aid program with CPR and keep your certification up to date. Hopefully you will never need to use the skills that you have acquired, but there is no better way to keep them sharply tuned than to continue to practise, roleplay, and think proactively about both your safety and the safety of the children trusted to your care.

This workbook has been revied by Active Canadian Emergency Training Inc., and serves as a reference. This workbook does not replace firstaid certification. It is the reader's responsibility to maintain current first aid/CPR certification. The material in this manual is "as printed" and carries  no guarantee. Every effort as been made to ensure accuracy, but neither the authors nor the publishers, or Active Canadian Emergency Training Inc., shall have any liability to any party with respect to loss or damage caused or alleged to be caused directly or indirectly by the instructions contained in this manual.

NOTES

_____

_____

_____

_____

_____

_____

_____

_____

_____

_____

_____

_____

_____

_____

REVIEW QUESTIONS

1. An emergency is
a. television not working
b. forgetting to do your homework
c. a serious situation that happens unexpectedly and demands immediate attention
d. losing your bicycle

2. An example of a medical emergency is someone trying to break into the house.
a. true
b. false

3. What should you do at the start of your babysitting job to help prevent accidents?
a. complete your Safety Checklist
b. remove all items that may be choking hazards
c. identify danger zones inside and outside the home
d. all of the above

4. What should you consider taking to become a skilled responder to first-aid emergencies?
a. watch movies and learn what to do in emergencies
b. read a book about first aid
c. nothing, a babysitter's training program is all I need
d. take a certified first aid and CPR program

5. Describe what you should do if a child has swallowed a small object and is coughing and choking.

encourage the child to cough and give support

6. What are some causes of a child having difficulty breathing?
a. asthma
b. allergies
c. choking
d. all of the above

7. What are some causes of anaphylactic shock?
a. allergies
b. walking up and scaring someone
c. falling off your bike
d. dehydration

8. What should you do if someone has a complete blockage?
a. abdominal thrusts
b. call 911
c. tell the child to stay calm
d. all of the above

9. Name one way that you can prevent a child from choking.

Properly cut food

10. Choose the correct answer:

☑ c cuts

☑ a punctures

☑ b scrapes

a. injuries that stab into the skin
b. injuries to the top part of your skin
c. injuries that slice the skin open

11. What should you do to stop a cut from bleeding?

Put pressure on it

12. You are babysitting an 8-year-old boy. He slips on some mud outside and falls and hits his head on the sidewalk. He is a bit dizzy, vomits, and seems to suddenly be tired. What should you do?

Call 9-1-1 and the parents

13. List the burn types in order from worst to least severe.
• third-degree
• first-degree
• second-degree

14. If you get a first- or second-degree burn, you should immediately put butter on it.
a. true
b. false

15. The best way to treat a first- or second-degree burn is to apply a cool damp cloth or water to the affected area.

a. true

b. false

16. Whom should you call if you feel that a child has become poisoned?

Poisson Control

NOTES

Conclusion

Congratulations! You have completed *The Babysitter's Handbook!* You are now much more prepared to become not only a good babysitter—but a great babysitter!

You have developed skills that will

• help you find and prepare for a babysitting job

• help you care for kids of all ages and deal with difficult situations

• help you prepare safe and fun activities for the kids you babysit

• help you make safe choices while babysitting and on your own

• help you predict future dangerous situations and know what to do in an emergency

• help you deal with concerns about possible abuse or neglect of children.

We recommend you enroll in a Kidproof Babysitter's Training Program and a certified first-aid program prior to babysitting. If you can't locate a program in your area, visit **www.kidproofsafety.com** to find out more about the Advanced Kidproof Babysitter's Training and Home Study Program.

Thank you and good luck in the future!

Further Training

Now you can go beyond the book and get more instruction in Kidproof Safety's Advanced Babysitter's Training Program! If you want to learn more about how to build a great babysitter clientele, how to care for several kids and babies, this course is for you!

Kidproof-trained babysitters are the very best—safe, reliable, and in demand!

To enroll in a Kidproof Babysitter's Training Program today, visit WWW.KIDPROOFSAFETY.COM

NOTES

Definitions and Forms

Allergy: An abnormally high sensitivity to certain substances such as pollens and foods.

Baby monitor: An electronic device used to transmit sounds when you are not in the room.

Baby wipes: Clean moist towels to wash a baby.

Babysitter's kit: A bag or knapsack full of items that you will need on your babysitting job.

Babysitter's rate: The amount that you will charge to babysit.

Bassinet: An oblong basket-like bed for an infant.

Bottle nipple: The rubber cap on a bottle from which a baby nurses.

Carbon monoxide: A colourless, odourless, highly poisonous gas.

Client: The person that you hope to work for.

Colicky: Suffering from excessive gas.

Cradle: A baby bed with sides and rockers.

Diaper rash: Soreness and redness on the skin of the thighs and buttocks of infants.

Emergency contact list: A list of emergency numbers and contact information you will need from the parents.

Employer: The person who hires you to do a job.

Fire escape plan: A planned escape route from different parts of a house used in case of a fire.

Formula: A liquid food for infants containing most of the nutrients in human milk.

Friction: The rubbing of one object or surface against another.

Letters of reference: Letters from people who recommend you and can speak about your experiences and skills.

Lukewarm: Moderately warm, not hot, tepid.

Separation anxiety: Excessive and persistent anxiety about being separated from one's home or parents that interferes with normal activities.

Toilet-roll test: If an object can fit inside a toilet paper roll, it is small enough to be a choking hazard.

Client Information Sheet

(Keep this form to record all future babysitting jobs with this client.*)

Name:_____

Phone number: _____

Address: _____

Number of children: _____

Name   Age

_____   _____

_____   _____

_____   _____

Number and type of pets:_____

Job Information

Hourly rate: _____

How I get to and from the job: _____

_____

*See Interview Questions for more specific information.

Date of Job	Paid	Notes

DEFINITIONS AND FORMS

Interview Questions

Date and time of interview: _____

Name of client: _____

Phone number: _____

Cell phone number: _____

Address: _____

Job Information

Date of job: _____

Start time:_____ End time: _____

Number of children: _____

Name   **Age**

_____   _____

_____   _____

_____   _____

Number and type of pets:_____

Hourly rate: _____

Questions

(Save this sheet and put it with your Client Information Sheet for future reference.)

How do I get to and from the job?

May I meet your children and pets before babysitting?

Will I be taking care of the pets?

Will I be preparing any meals or snacks?

Do your children have any allergies or take any medications?

Do your children have any special needs?

Do you have a fire escape plan?

What are your children's favourite foods?

What are their favourite games and activities?

Emergency Phone List
(to be completed by the parents/guardians)

Name of client(s): _____

Where we will be: _____

Expected return time: _____

Phone number: _____

Cell phone number: _____

Neighbour's name: _____

Neighbour's phone number: _____

Neighbour's location: _____

Emergency number: 911

Other: _____

Our home address: _____

Our fire number (if applies): _____

Nearest landmark: _____

_____

Number of children: _____

Name   **Age**

_____ _____

_____ _____

_____ _____

_____ _____

_____ _____

Allergies or medications:

_____

_____

_____

_____

_____

Poison control centre: _____

Safety Checklist

(Ask parents/guardians if they will take you for a tour of the house.)

1. Emergency Phone List and Rules and
   Routines List are completed.

2. I know the location of the following items:
First-aid kit location: _____

Flashlights location: _____

Fire extinguisher location: _____

Fire alarm location: _____

(Check with parents to make sure these are in working order.)

3. The areas children are not allowed in:

_____

_____

4. I know the fire escape plan.
   The children know the fire escape plan.

5. Safety gates are in place (if this applies).

6. Doors and windows are locked.

7. Outside lights are on (if applies).

DEFINITIONS AND FORMS

8. The house alarm is on (if applies).
   I know the procedure if the house alarm goes off.

9. I have checked all rooms for potential hazards.
   Potentially dangerous items have been removed from each room.

10. Additional safety information:

_____

_____

_____

_____

_____

_____

_____

_____

_____

_____

_____

Rules and Routines Checklist

General Rules and Routimes

1. What are the household rules?

_____

_____

2. How would you like me to handle misbehaviour?

_____

_____

3. Is there any separation anxiety? What helps ease it?

_____

_____

4. Are there any chores that need to be completed?

_____

_____

5. Is there any homework that the children need to do?

_____

6. Do they have any music or sports practices?

_____

_____

7. May I use the telephone, television, or video equipment?

_____

Bedtime Routines

1. What are the children's bedtimes?

_____

2. Are there any routines for

brushing their teeth: _____

putting pyjamas on (also know where the pyjamas are):

_____

other: _____

3. Do they have any bedtime routines?
   - ☐ rock them to sleep
   - ☐ have a night light
   - ☐ sleep with a soother
   - ☐ leave the door open or closed
   - ☐ have a special toy

☐ read a story before bed

☐ other: _____

4. Do they ever have nightmares? If so, how do you handle them?

_____

_____

Pet Routines

1. Do you have any pets that I will be taking care of?

_____

_____

2. Where is the pet food?

_____

_____

3. Is there a pet door or do I need to let the pet out?

_____

_____

Play Routines

1. Are there certain clothes that you would like the children to wear if they are playing outside? If so, where are they located?

_____

_____

_____

2. Where does dirty clothing go?

_____

3. Do I need to put sunscreen lotion or insect repellant on your children when they play outside?

_____

4. What are your children's favourite games and activities?

_____

_____

Eating Routines
(Make sure that any allergies/medications are noted on the Emergency Phone List.)

1. Will I be preparing any meals or snacks?

_____

2. What are your children's favourite foods?

_____

3. Do your children have any routines for eating?

_____

_____

Additional Information

1. Are there any additional rules and routines that I should know about?

_____

_____

(If your clients have a baby or toddler, ask them the baby or toddler questions now.)

Additional Rules and Routines

Baby Care Questions (0–1 year)

1. What do I feed the baby?

_____

2. Where do I feed the baby?

_____

3. When do I feed the baby?

_____

4. Is the baby a fussy eater? What do I do if the baby makes a fuss when eating?

_____

_____

5. Is the baby teething? What do I do for that?

_____

6. What is your diapering routine?

_____

7. What do you do for a diaper rash?

_____

Toddler Care Questions (1–3 years)

1. Is the toddler still in diapers or toilet training?

_____

2. If still in diapers, what is the diapering routine?

_____

3. If toilet training, what is the toilet routine?

_____

4. Are there any problems with bedwetting?

_____

5. Where are the clean bedding and clean clothing kept?

_____

Report Card

(to be completed by the babysitter and reviewed with the parents/guardians)

We had the most fun when

_____

_____

_____

_____

The children's behaviour was

☐ very good

☐ good

☐ some behaviour issues

The children were very good at

_____

_____

_____

_____

_____

I handled the misbehaviour by

_____

_____

_____

_____

We ate (type of food)_____

_____

at (time) _____

The children went to bed at _____

_____

_____

You had the following phone calls. We did not answer the phone unless we heard the code ring (as previously arranged).

Time   **Phone Number** (if caller ID available)

_____   _____

_____   _____

_____   _____

_____   _____

_____   _____

You had _____ visitors to the door.

We did not answer the door unless it was _____,
who you had told us would be visiting.

He/she came by at _____

We had the following accidents:

Time _____

Type of accident _____

What I did to help_____

_____

Time _____

Type of accident _____

What I did to help_____

_____

Time _____

Type of accident _____

What I did to help_____

_____

_____

My favourite part of this job was

_____

_____

_____

_____

_____

Other comments:

_____

_____

_____

_____

_____

_____

_____

_____

Answer Keys

SECTION ONE
Becoming a Great Babysitter

1. There is no legal age to babysit. In most States there is no law that states when a child can legally babysit and there is no such thing as a "babysitter's license."

2. Kids mature and learn at different speeds. Because of this, there is no law that says you must be a certain age to babysit. If there was, some kids might be babysitting before they are mature enough to do so.

3. (e)
4. (b)
5. (b), (d)
6. (b), (d)
7. (b)
8. (a), (b)
9. (c)
10. (b)
11. Never accept a babysitting job when you are not qualified to ensure the child's, and your own, safety. Even if parents are desperate for a babysitter, you will have to tell them that you do not feel you will be able to care for their child properly, and decline the offer. If you know of another babysitter who may be more experienced or skilled, you may offer to contact him or her. Great babysitters are able to recognize their limitations.
12. e, b, a, d, c

SECTION TWO
Preparing for Your Babysitting Job.

1. (e)
2.
• brings lots of fun games
• is nice
• plays with them
3.
• The babysitter is reliable.
• The babysitter is trustworthy.
• The babysitter is safe.
4. (c)
5. (a)
6. (d)
7. Take the time after they leave to walk through the house and note any safety hazards. Take the children with you and make a game of it. Ask them if they can see any safety hazards. If you see areas of concern, remove them or close them off in a room.

Insist that the parents provide you with an emergency phone number in case you need them to answer any questions that they did not have time to cover upon your arrival.

If you are asked to babysit in the future, remind the parents that you would like to spend a few minutes before they leave going over house rules.
8. a, b, c

SECTION THREE
Having a Successful Babysitting Experience

1. (a)
2. (d)
3. (a)
4. (a)
5. (b)
6. (b)
7. crib, high chair, stroller, portable car seat

8. (b)
9. (b)
10. (b)
11. (a)
12. (a)
13. (d)
14. (a)
15. (d)
16. (b)
17. colouring book and crayons
18. (b)
19. i, a, b, c, d, h, e, f, g

SECTION FOUR
Safety
1. (a)
2. (d)
3. (b)
4. (a)
5. (c)
6. (a)
7. (a)
8. (a)
9. (d)
10. (a)
11. b, a

SECTION FIVE
Abuse, Neglect, and Protecting Kids
1. (b)
2. (b)
3. (c)
4. (a)
5. (a)

SECTION SIX
Babysitter's First Aid
1. (c)
2. (b)
3. (d)
4. (d)
5. If the child is coughing, it means that there is some air passing and therefore is only a partial blockage. It is best to encourage the child to continue to cough. Never leave the child alone; the partial blockage could easily become a full blockage and the child will not be able to breathe. DO NOT pat the child on the back. Simply encourage him or her to continue coughing until the partial blockage is cleared.
6. (d)
7. (a)
8. (d)
9. Do not let children jump around or play while they are eating.
10. c, a, b
11. Apply constant pressure and if possible, raise the cut above heart level.
12. The child is showing signs of a concussion and head injury. Do not let him go to sleep. Immediately Call 911 and stay by his side until paramedics arrive.
13. third-degree, second-degree, first-degree
14. (b)
15. (a)
16. The poison control centre. You can find the phone number in the front of your phone book.

E.M.S.

What is E.M.S.?

Emergency Medical Services

When do I call E.M.S.?

Emergency situation that requires the help of a police officer, paramedic, or firefighter

What do I tell E.M.S.?

- Your location
- The type of emergency
- If there are any Injuries
- Who the victim is (age, medications, etc.)
- What is being done to help?

DON'T HANG UP UNTIL THEY TELL YOU TO!

Fire

What Should You Do in a Fire?

1. Get out of the house first and don't stop for any personal items or pets. If there is smoke, get down on your knees and crawl (smoke rises so you need to get as close to the ground as possible, where the air is cleaner).

2. Run to a neighbour's house and call 9-1-1.

3. If you can't get past the fire, close the doors between you and the fire. Touch the door before opening it. If it is hot, do not open it. Call for help.

4. If your clothing is on fire, STOP, DROP AND ROLL. Stop immediately, drop to the ground and cover your face with your hands and roll on the ground. Keep rolling until the fire is out. Do not run!

5. Smother the flames with a blanket or a jacket while the child is on the ground.

6. Wait outside for the fire department to arrive. Tell them if there is a pet inside the house.

Kidproof
Knowledge is the key

First Aid 1

Kidproof
Knowledge is the key

Cuts & Scrapes

1. Clean around the wound with soap and water (or an antiseptic wipe if you have one available).

2. Use a sterile bandage or clean cloth and apply pressure onto the cut to stop the bleeding. Do not put pressure if there is glass or another object in the cut.

3. Continue applying pressure for up to 10 minutes if you need to. Use a sterile bandage or clean cloth.

4. Hold the injury higher than the heart (this slows blood flow to that spot).

5. Put one or more band-aids on the cut.

Treatment for Cuts

• Put the band-aid across the cut so it can help hold the cut together.

• The sides of the cut skin should touch, but not overlap.

• Don't touch the cut with your hand.

Nosebleeds

Treatment

1. Sit the child down and have the child lean forward.

2. Using Kleenex or a sterile cloth pinch the nostrils shut. Gently squeeze using your thumb and forefinger.

3. Hold for 15 uninterrupted minutes. Tell the child to breathe through their mouth.

4. Continue to hold the cloth until the bleeding slows to a stop. This may take up to fifteen minutes, so be patient.

5. Once the bleeding stops make sure that the child does not blow his nose for at least 24 hours and choose a quiet play activity.

6. If the nose is bleeding very heavily, or is a result of a fall or head injury, call 911.

- Unconsciousness, contusion or drowsiness.
- Inability to move any part of the body or weakness in an arm or leg.
- Dent, bruise, cut or blood on the scalp.
- Severe headache.
- Stiff neck.
- Vomiting.
- Blood or fluid that comes from the mouth, nose or ears.
- Loss of vision, blurred or double vision, pupils of unequal size.
- Convulsions.

Treatment

- If the child has fallen YOU MUST advise the parents.
- Even if they appear to be fine, parents need to know of the incident so that they can keep a close eye on symptoms over the next 24 hours.
- Bleeding in the brain often starts within the first 24 hours after a head injury and can last for three days or longer.
- If necessary, call 911.

1. Make a bandage from gauze and first-aid tape. Cuts
2. If the bleeding is very heavy and does not stop with simple pressure and rest (ie. the cut is still bleeding for more than 20 minutes), call 911. Keep pressure on the wound while you wait for help.
3. Some cuts are deep enough that they require stitching or gluing shut and immediate medical attention. Call 911.
4. Be sure to advise the parents of the injury and the reasons as soon as they return home.

Treatment for Punctures

1. Do not move or attempt to remove the object.
2. Call 911 and wait for the E.M.S.

First Aid 2

Kidproof
Knowledge is the key

	First Degree Burns	Second Degree Burns	Third Degree Burns
Layer of Skin Affected	• Outer layer of your skin.	• Lower layers and outer skin.	• Outer and deep layers of skin, underlying tissue and organs. • Most serious burns.
Appearance	• Burned area can by dry, red, slightly swollen. • Painful and sensitive to touch. • Example: mild sunburn.	• Painful, swollen, and shows redness and blisters. • Skin develops a watery surface. • Can be very painful. • Example: severe sunburn.	• Appear black and white, charred, skin swollen, underlying tissue often exposed. • May not be as painful as first or second degree - if burn destroyed nerve endings, may be no pain at all. • Example: electrical shock.
Treatment	• Do apply cool cloth or water to affected area.	• First aid treatment possible	• Always requires emergency

- If arms or legs burned, elevate above heart level.
- Cover burned area with clear cloth or sterile dressing - don't use plastic.
- Should heal in about a week.

Burns

The Severity of a Burn is Based On:

- How deep the burn is (how many layers of skin are burned).
- How much of the body is burned.
- Where the burn is on the body.

Poisons

Treatment

- If the child is conscious, call the Poison Control Center immediately. Try to determine the cause of the poisoning. If the child inhaled a poison, remove them from the toxic air.
- If the child is unconscious, you must immediately call 911 and perform artificial respiration as learned in a certified First Aid and CPR program.
- If you know the cause of the poisoning, give the Poison Control Center as much information as you can.

  1. Name, make of product.
  2. If the product was swallowed, inhaled, or came in contact with skin.
  3. How much of the product was taken.
  4. Details such as age and symptoms of the child.

- Follow the instructions given to you by the Poison Control Center.

First Aid 3

Kidproof
Knowledge is the key

Choking

Partial Blockage

- The item is only partially blocking the airway.
- If the child is coughing and choking, then it is a partial blockage.
- If they are able to cough, then air is getting through.
- Encourage them to keep coughing.

Complete blockage

- The item is completely blocking the airway.
- When a complete blockage has occurred NO air is passing through.
- You must react IMMEDIATELY. Call 9-1-1, then begin performing abdominal thrusts.

Children (over one-year-old)

Anaphylactic Shock

This is a type of reaction from allergic exposure.

Causes

- Insect bites or stings
- Nuts
- Food allergies

What Happens

- Begins within minutes of exposure to substance causing the allergy.
- Airways narrow and make it very difficult to breathe.
- Can kill if a person with 15 minutes, if not treated.

Signs & Symptoms

- Difficulty breathing
- Swollen tongue, eyes or face
- Unconsciousness

- Immediately call 9-1-1.
- Follow procedures the parents demonstrated.
- Remove item that caused the allergic reaction.
- Comfort the child and monitor their breathing until EMS arrives.

Asthma

Asthma means the inside walls of your airway are swollen. The inflammation makes the airways very sensitive, and they will react to irritants by narrowing and then less air will flow into your lungs.

Symptoms of an asthmatic reaction:

- Whistling sound when you breathe.
- Coughing.
- Chest Tightness.
- Trouble Breathing.

Prevention:

If you are babysitting a child with asthma, be sure that you clearly understand the treatment and limits that you will need to follow. Some children may have asthma as an allergic reaction; some may find their asthma is worse when they have a cold or physically exert themselves – ask the parents!

Treatment:

For most children, asthma is controlled through inhalers and other medications. Be sure to note proper procedures that the parents have given you on your rules and routines sheet.

- Pull your fists in and up tightly in the shape of the letter "J".
- Continue this motion with as much force as necessary until the item is pushed from the airway or EMS arrives.

Infant (under one-year-old)

- If you are caring for an infant that is under one-year-old, you must consider taking a certified First Aid course to build confidence and the skills required to perform rescue breathing if necessary.

- We do not recommend that anyone (adult or youth) babysit an infant without current certified First Aid training.

- Check your local hospital or First Aid provider for a class near you before considering caring for an infant unsupervised.

Kidproof
Knowledge is the key

Golden Rules

TO FIND A GREAT BABYSITTING JOB!

1. Always get permission from your parents before accepting any babysitting job. It is your parents' final decision whether you will be able to babysit. Make them part of the decision process.

2. Never answer or post babysitting job advertisements. It is dangerous to answer an ad looking for a babysitter. You do not know the person who is posting the ad, nor do you know the kids. ONLY babysit for family, friends and neighbors that you and your parents already know.

3. Never place an ad or post a notice in a public area like a library or recreation center saying

Three Step Preparation Plan

One week prior

1. Check contents in babysitting kit and make activity plan.

2. Make copies of all forms needed including Safety Checklist, Rules and Routines Checklist, and Report Card.

3. Call the client to confirm.

be babysitting until, how you are getting home, contact name and info.

2. Complete homework

3. Tell your friends that you are not available that night. DO NOT GIVE THEM THE PHONE NUMBER TO YOUR JOB.

4. Review your interview and follow up questions. Make notes to any questions that you will still need answered the day of the job.

Day of the job

1. Arrive at least 15 minutes early. *If it is the first time that you are babysitting for the family, ask if you can come about ½ hour early.

2. Complete the Safety Checklist and Rules and Routines Checklist.

3. Review your Emergency Contact list.

4. HAVE FUN!

5. Never register for a babysitters' group or through an organization that claims to find babysitting jobs. The BEST way to find a babysitting job is to go to people that you already know!

TIPS FOR TAKING CARE

BABIES (0-1 YEARS OLD)

- Need to be held and feel like they are loved and not alone.
- Need 100% of our time and attention.
- Some love to be held; others want to sit alone and watch everything.
- Take the time to learn about what each baby likes and dislikes—the best way is to ask the parents.

SPECIFIC BABY QUESTIONS TO ASK THE PARENTS

1. What do I feed the baby?
2. Where do I feed the baby?
3. When do I feed the baby?
4. Is the baby a fussey eater? What do I do if the baby makes a fuss when eating?
5. Is the baby teething? What do I do for that?
6. What is your diapering routine?
7. What do you do for a diaper rash?

PRESCHOOLERS (3-5 YEARS)

- Have very clear ideas of what they like and dislike.
- Love individual attention.
- Like to make decisions; give them choices when picking a snack or activity.
- Enjoy doing puzzles, playing with a ball.
- Like to dress up and pretend.

SCHOOL-AGE (5+)

- Great age to babysit for a new babysitter.
- Play with them.
- Set a good example by your actions and reactions to them and your surroundings.
- Be fair and positive.
- Do not "tell" them what to do, but make suggestions.
- Be firm when applying safety rules, but find fun and interesting ways to deal with their everyday chores.

- Love to make things and build things.
- Like doing what you are doing (i.e. if you are washing dishes, let them help out).

SPECIFIC TODDLER QUESTIONS TO ASK THE PARENTS

1. Is the toddler still in diapers or toilet training?
2. If still in diapers, what is the diapering routine?
3. If toilet training, what is the toilet routine?
4. Are there any problems with bedwetting?
5. Where is the clean bedding and clean clothing kept?

6-8 YEAR-OLDS

- Can play alone, draw, or create without constant attention.
- Love stories.
- Like active play (sports with friends).

8-10 YEAR-OLDS

- Can play or do homework without constant attention.
- Can play more complex games.
- More independent, may resist assistance.
- Require supervision although they may feel they don't.

With all age groups, it is best to have the parents explain the rules in front of the children so they know they can't fool you later!

Kidproof

Knowledge is the key

TIPS FOR TAKING CARE

FEEDING FACTS

Ask Parents About

- Food they should eat
- Dislikes and allergies

ALWAYS

- Wash yours and the child's hands
- Have children sit still
- Supervise while eating
- Clean up and get kids to help

FEEDING A TODDLER

- Check the temperature of any foods that require heating up
- Buckle into high chair and never leave them unattended
- Make sure dangerous items are not within reach
- Cut food into bite sized pieces that are easy to chew

DRESSING FOR SUCCESS!

BABY

- May have to change clothes a couple of times if they spit up or have a diaper leak.
- Protect the baby's head by supporting it with your hand.
- Be careful with the baby's arms.
- Do not overdress a baby - if you are comfortable with a t-shirt on, they will be too. If the baby is outside and sitting in a stroller, they may need a blanket to keep them warm since they are not moving around like you are.
- When outside, baby must always have a hat on.
- Babies cannot wear sunscreen, so keep them in the shade.
- If it's really cold outside, don't take the baby outside.

TODDLER

- May get quite dirty

- Avoid hard foods like carrots and meat (can become a choking hazard)

FEEDING SCHOOL-AGED KIDS

- Have activity the child can do while you are preparing the meal
- When possible let children choose their meal or snack. They like to make decisions too!

PRE-SCHOOL

- Should be able to dress themselves, but will still need assistance with zippers, snaps, and lace tying.
- If resisting getting dressed, make it a game e.g.: "Find your yellow jacket." or "Find your blue shoes."
- Let them help decide what they should wear.
- May have definite ideas about what they want to wear. Use your judgement as to whether the clothing they choose to wear is appropriate or not.

SCHOOL-AGE

- Capable of dressing themselves and choosing appropriate clothing.
- If going outside, make note of whether they have appropriate clothing on for the weather outside, and make suggestions as necessary.

Kidproof
Knowledge is the key

TIPS FOR TAKING CARE

4 STEP ACTION PLAN

In any emergency, it is vital that you stay calm, think and act logically. To respond safely to an emergency, learn and apply a Four Step Emergency Action Plan.

1. ASSESS THE SITUATION

First assess the situation and the surroundings. Look at the situation clearly. The answers to these questions will determine your next course of action.

Consider:
- How did the accident/emergency happen?
- Is there anyone injured?
- Is there any imminent danger?
- Is there anyone else that may help?

2. SAFETY

Assess the safety of responding; it is vital that you consider the safety of you and others around you before initiating

ALL WORK NO PLAY!

THE BEST WAY TO SUPERVISE CHILDREN IS TO PLAY WITH THEM!

PLAYTIME WITH BABY

- Best time to play with a baby is after feeding and changing
- Babies love attention; respond to musical sounds, rattles & squeaks
- Only give babies large soft toys - nothing that can break apart and become small enough to fit into their mouth
- If they drop a toy, wash and rinse it off before giving it back to the baby (everything goes into a baby's mouth).
- Have the parents show you what toys are the baby's favorites

PLAYTIME WITH TODDLERS

- Toddlers love to keep busy! They love stories and games

when you leave).

- Toddlers love to put things in their mouth, nose, and ears; remove any objects you feel the toddler could choke on or put inside his body.

PLAYTIME WITH PRE-SCHOOLERS

- This age group is curious and can be demanding
- They understand what "NO" means and will often challenge it. Stick to your decisions and clearly set out the rules and guidelines to them.
- They love active games, and anything physical.
- Try to include appropriate safe toys in your kit to surprise them with something different from their regular toys.

PLAYTIME WITH SCHOOL AGE

- Even though school aged kids are more independent, they still need to be supervised; they are more likely to have an accidental injury than toddlers and babies.
- Go with them everywhere. Be cautious of traffic and follow all bicycle safety rules such as always wearing a helmet.
- Bring some games and activities with you (may be different from what the child has).

Kidproof®

Knowledge is the key

- If possible, remove danger from the injured person.
  - Only move the injured person if it is safe to do so.

3. TREAT THE MOST SERIOUS INJURY FIRST

If you are faced with an emergency that has more than one person injured, it is important to determine which person has the most serious and treatable injury.

Consider:

- Always treat the most serious, injury first. If you are treating a child, remember that the two most life threatening conditions are the inability to breathe and serious bleeding.

4. CALL FOR HELP

If possible, be sure to call for help before starting First Aid. From the time you initially assessed the situation, you should have called for help, or requested someone to do so for you.

Consider:

- You can call 9-1-1 from any cell phone or pay phone free of charge.
- Call for help before you begin First Aid